Leslie Adatto

111 Rooftops in New York That You Must Not Miss

Photographs by Clay Williams

D0063838

emons:

Did you enjoy this guidebook? Would you like to see more?
Join us in uncovering new places around the world on:
www.111places.com

Foreword

New York is my boyfriend.

As soon as I was able to leave the maddening, drive-everywhere Southern California lifestyle, I packed up my oversized suitcase and little computer, shipped my dog and my bike, and moved across the country to be, at long last, with my true love, New York City.

When I got here, I looked for the most romantic experiences we could have together, and I found that rooftops, elevated above street level by a little or a lot, made the City look oh-so-sparkly, smart, and handsome. Just high enough above the grit and noise of the weathered street grid, it turns out, New York City looks its absolute best, whether at one of the many bars, swinging on a hammock at a rooftop winery, touring an elevated high-tech farm, swimming 25 feet above the Hudson River, ice-skating under a rooftop bubble, or watching an outdoor film in the sky. The possibilities seemed endless, so I continued exploring new ways to experience this alluring, romantic side of New York City.

Speaking practically, rooftops are the last bastion of undeveloped real estate in New York, so turning them into something special makes so much sense in this densely populated metropolis. Speaking from the heart, looking down on the city just makes it that much more alluring, like a sparkling jewel surrounded by crystal waters.

Hundreds of rooftops and thousands of bicycle miles later, I was asked to share this way of experiencing the country's most populous and popular city with you, so *111 Rooftops That You Must Not Miss* was created. I hope you too will see New York City from an entirely new, softer, quieter, much more romantic perspective that its vast and varied array of publically accessible rooftops affords.

Though New York is my boyfriend, we are far from exclusive; New York can easily be your boyfriend – or girlfriend – too! Enjoy the romance it offers all year round from 111 of its most enchanting rooftops.

111 Rooftops

1__1 Rooftop Garden & Bar

Three ways to enjoy the balmy summertime

Between May and October, New York City boasts sunny days and balmy nights. So treat yourself to the rooftop that has just about everything: 1 Rooftop Garden & Bar in the trendy DUMBO neighborhood of Brooklyn.

Choose from three ways to enjoy this rooftop. The self-service area near the bar has tables with black-and-white shade umbrellas and cushioned stadium seating on huge wooden beams salvaged from the nearby Domino Sugar factory. On the roof's south side are large upholstered benches where wait staff serve drinks and small plates. Beyond that is the three-foot-deep splash pool deck dotted with comfy daybeds. Weekend pool parties are open to the public, and day passes are available.

The outdoor shower by the pool is backed by a vine-covered mesh wall, and the plantings throughout are varied and informal, with everything from trees to flowering bushes, much like Brooklyn Bridge Park below. A standout sculpture created by a local artist adorns one of the planters, and the subtle lighting scheme makes this roof even more inviting at nighttime.

The views of Governors Island, New York Harbor, boats motoring up the East River, the lights of the skyscrapers in Manhattan, and the majestic Brooklyn Bridge are just about perfect from this eleventh-story perch, high enough to see the grand vista but close enough to note details of the park, river, and city below.

Perfection comes with a price, and at 1 Rooftop Garden & Bar, that translates into a strong suggestion to make an advanced reservation. If the roof is at capacity, there is an indoor sister bar, The Brooklyn Heights Social Club, on the tenth floor. This comfortable lounge with DJ or live music offers the same views year-round through floor-to-ceiling windows, but on the perfect summer New York City evening, the best choice is always upstairs on the roof.

Address 1 Hotel Brooklyn Bridge, 60 Furman Street, 11th Floor, Brooklyn, NY 11201, +1 (347)696-2505, www.1hotels.com/brooklyn-bridge/taste/1-rooftop-garden-bar | **Getting there** Subway to High Street (Line A, C), to Clark Street (Line 2, 3), or bus B 25 to Old Fulton Street / Elizabeth Place | **Hours** Mon–Fri 4pm–midnight, Sat & Sun noon–midnight | **Tip** Get cultural at the nearby St Ann's Warehouse, a cutting-edge theater built inside a Civil War-era tobacco warehouse (45 Water Street, Brooklyn, NY 11201, www.stannswarehouse.org).

2   5-Boro Green Roof Garden

35 green roof systems on one spectacular rooftop

"Example isn't another way to teach, it is the only way to teach."
Albert Einstein's pearl of wisdom is true even in the sprouting green
roof industry. We know that green roofs are a good idea, but which
type absorbs the most water, requires the least water, grows edibles,
or sustains larger plants? These and multitudes more questions are
being answered by the New York City Parks Department at the largest multi-system green roof on the planet.

On Randall's Island, atop the Five Borough Administration Building, 35 different green roof systems covering 30,000 square feet grow
side by side on the 5-Boro Green Roof Garden.

Different types and depths of growing media are planted with
native plants, a variety of sedum, fruits, vegetables, herbs, and berries. There is a hydroponic system and solar. Italian honey bees buzz
around happily pollinating the plants. Up to 6,000 gallons of rainwater overflow is captured in barrels to reduce storm water runoff
and used later to irrigate. The data helps determine what works best.

This living roof is a lush, park-like setting for bipeds (that's us) to
spend time enjoying views of the East River, the Triborough (Robert
F. Kennedy) Bridge, and the unique vistas only available from this
island-bound green roof laboratory nestled between Manhattan,
Queens, and the Bronx.

Since 2007, in response to Mayor Bloomberg's comprehensive
sustainability plan, the Parks Department began with its first green
roof. Each year, under the loving care of Artie Rollins, Assistant
Commissioner of Citywide Services for the Parks Department, and
his attentive staff, another carefully chosen green roof system or two
is added to expand data collection.

Accessible only by prearranged tour, and with limited bus service
to Randall's Island, this must-see destination is for roof explorers who
are excellent planners and in no rush.

Address New York City Parks Department Five Borough Administration Building, 20 Bronx Shore Road, Randall's Island, NY 10035, +1 (212)360-8905, www.nycgovparks.org/greening/sustainable-parks/green-roofs | Getting there Subway to 125 Street (Line 4, 5, 6), or bus M 35 to Main Roadway / Opposite Park & Recreation | Hours By appointment only | Tip The absolute best way to see Randall's Island is on its eight miles of car-free bike paths. About a mile below the pedestrian bridge to the island, rent a bike at Danny's Cycles UES (1690 Second Avenue, NY 10128, www.dannyscycles.com/about/upper-east-side).

3 _ A+ Roof Bar
Chinatown's anti-corporate hotel roof bar

New York City's hotel rooftop bars are often deep-pocket operations designed by top interior decorators, staffed by corporate hospitality professionals, and publicized by agencies with social media experts. A delightful exception to this rule, however, is the A+ Roof Bar in Flushing, at the edge of Queens' rapidly growing Chinatown. Located on the thirteenth floor of the Parc Hotel, A+ Roof Bar is anything but corporate.

The décor is unusual. Walls full of stickers greet guests as they exit the elevator, the neon wall sconces sporting drinking phrases are blindingly blue and brash, and the curio cabinet adorned with kitsch looks like something from grandma's house. Yet the over-the-bar lighting is calming, the upscale bar is furnished with inviting chairs, and excellent jazz plays at a volume that is perfect for creating a relaxed mood and encouraging conversation.

A+ Roof Bar manages to meld three distinct areas in a fairly small footprint. The lounge, furnished with bench-style couches that suit a small group, is a little sunroom. The interior bar strives for an old-time, stylish ambience. The outside terrace is small, but the nighttime lights make it spectacular. A dozen or so wooden bar stools and a parapet with a built-in ledge on which to rest a drink invites guests to watch planes take off and land at LaGuardia Airport or peer into Citi Field. The last stretch of the 7 subway line lies below, as is the constant stream of traffic on the Whitestone Expressway. The lights of Manhattan and the Throgs Neck Bridge twinkle in the distance.

Drinks are handcrafted with house-made ingredients, such as bacon-fat-washed rum in the Dark Plum libation, or sherry *sous-vide* with osmanthus, an East Asian flower, in the Osmanthus cocktail. The daily happy hour offers buy-one-get-one-free specials, while the sunsets from the west-facing terrace are thrown in for free.

Address Parc Hotel, 39-16 College Point Boulevard, Level R, Queens, NY 11354, www.theparchotel.com/dining, roofbaraplus@gmail.com | **Getting there** Subway to Flushing–Main Street (Line 7), or bus Q48 to Roosevelt Avenue/College Point Boulevard | **Hours** Daily 5:30pm–2am | **Tip** Sip a delicious whipped cheese tea at the Taiwanese bubble tea shop Happy Lemon in Queens Crossing Food Hall (136-17 39th Avenue, Queens, NY 11354, www.queenscrossing.com).

4 __ Allora Alto

Northern Italian fare moves uptown & up on a roof

More than three decades spent working in Lower Manhattan's traditional Italian restaurants can teach you a thing or two about how to do things the right way.

Elio Albanese started as a busboy, learning the business from the inside out, and eventually donned the tuxedo and masterfully executed the role of maître d'. Elio is still looking very smart in his tuxedo, but now he wears it as the owner of several high-end Northern Italian restaurants.

In 2016, Mr. Albanese ventured out of his familiar Lower Manhattan neighborhood to Midtown East with Allora, which translates to, "What's next?" Elio's next move, in fact, was heading up to the 22nd floor in 2017 and creating the intimate Allora Alto on the open-air roof terrace. While it's a charming place to have drinks and light bites, such as fried calamari, bruschetta, or pizza, guests may order from the full menu. Unique to Allora is their famous 30-foot-long spaghetti and mini-meatballs dish. This specialty is an enormous swirl of continuous, handmade pasta that requires scissors to cut it – and four people to share it.

Allora Alto is cozy, with a few bistro and high-top tables and a couple of low couches with comfy cushions, as well as a small bar. Original artwork adorns one wall, while New York City's elegant art deco Chrysler Building rises directly ahead. The rest of the view is very typical for Manhattan's Midtown East neighborhood: lots of tall, close-knit, nondescript office buildings reminding guests at Allora Alto that they are unmistakably in Midtown Manhattan.

Twenty-two floors above the fray, this small bar is quiet enough for friends to engage in conversation while enjoying a glass of wine and some handmade Italian fare. Try Allora Alto while waiting for your table downstairs, or come up here to relax high above the bustle of business-centric Midtown in this hidden urban aerie.

Address 145 East 47th Street, 22nd Floor, New York, NY 10017, +1 (212)754-9800, www.alloranyc.com | Getting there Subway to 51st Street/Lexington Avenue (Line 6), to Grand Central–42nd Street (Line 4, 5, 6, 7, S), or bus M 102, M 103 to Third Avenue/ East 47th Street | Hours Daily 5–11pm in good weather | Tip For beautifully cut women's clothing made to fit from a local designer, shop at Gabrielle Carlson Studio (501 Lexington Avenue, New York, NY 10017, www.gabriellecarlson.com).

5 Alma

Well worth the journey

Looking for a cocktail and snack on a New York City rooftop? Lots of fun choices; just read the rest of this book! Trying to find an entire meal served on a rooftop in New York City? Not so easy. Fortunately, once again, gritty, industrial Brooklyn saves the day.

In 2002, long before the current rooftop craze, four partners literally built Alma, a three-tiered restaurant on the edge of Red Hook. Woodwork, tile work, glasswork – they did it all. On the ground floor they installed a neighborhood bar named after the B 61 bus that stops at the corner. Upstairs on the second floor is the kitchen and indoor seating for the restaurant.

Insiders, however, happily continue climbing up the few dozen stairs to the roof. Even though you may be coming off a tiring work week, each step is worthwhile, as you will be rewarded with one of those elusive full rooftop restaurants via Alma's rich and enticing menu. This attractive restaurant and bar serves delicious, affordable dinners and weekend brunch. It also graciously offers a sunset-saturated, memorable view of the Brooklyn Piers, New York Harbor, Governors Island, and the twinkling lights of Manhattan's skyscrapers.

Alma features Mexican cuisine, often with a creative twist. The *chilaquiles* (chewy strips of tortilla baked with melted cheese in a thin, spicy sauce) are an especially popular starter, and the *arroz con queso* (rice dressed up with poblano peppers and cheese) is a luscious and satisfying side dish to go with a selection of tasty main courses.

No reservations are taken for rooftop tables. On clear evenings when the retractable roof is flung wide open, these seats fill up fast, especially around sunset. Filled with neighborhood regulars, Alma's vibe is friendly, familiar, and welcoming. The rooftop is open all year round, with fresh air in the warmer months and ample heating when it gets cold outside.

Address 187 Columbia Street, Brooklyn, NY 11231, +1 (718)643-5400, www.almarestaurant.com | Getting there Subway to Carroll Street (Line F), or bus B 61 to Columbia Street/Sackett Street | Hours Mon–Thu 5:30–10pm, Fri 5–11pm, Sat 11am–11pm, Sun 11am–10pm | Tip Pier 6 at Brooklyn Bridge Park is the ultimate kids' playground headquarters with WaterLab, Slide Mountain, and the largest sandbox in New York City (daily, dawn–dusk; 334 Furman Street, Brooklyn, NY 11201, www.brooklynbridgepark.org/park/pier-6).

6_ Ample Hills Creamery
Summer's perfect combo – ice cream on a rooftop

Years before they made ice cream their business, Jackie Cuscuna, a native New Yorker, and her husband Brian Smith lived in an apartment that was too small. But they chose it because it had rooftop access, even if the only way up there was a ladder.

It's no surprise, then, that when searching for a home for their second Ample Hills Creamery ice cream factory and store, Jackie and Brian were entranced by a building in an industrial Brooklyn neighborhood because of its easy access to the roof. And so in 2014, Brooklyn's first ice cream roof deck was born.

During summer, rooftops have a magnetic pull, and ice cream shares this seasonal magnetism. Lucky for us, we can slurp, lick, and munch the completely made-from-scratch ice cream we've been dreaming about, while hanging out on a casual, colorful roof deck at Ample Hills Creamery in Gowanus.

Tables with umbrellas and a rainbow of painted Adirondack chairs adorn the rooftop. During the day, as parents socialize, toddlers play in the sandbox while they burn off their post-ice cream sugar rush. At night, strings of lights give this second-story rooftop a party-like atmosphere. The constantly changing crowd talks loudly over piped-in music, giving it a sophisticated outdoor bar feel, yet it's totally child friendly.

Though no alcohol is served here, it is easy to get drunk on the fun flavors that are all made in-house. With an array of irresistible flavors, such as Peppermint Pattie with house-made mint patties mixed in, and pretzel-infused ice cream that is the base of another creative flavor called The Munchies, deciding what to order can be excruciating! But the ice cream experts at Ample Hills Creamery have thought of everything. For about the price of two small cones, you can get a flight of six small scoops, each of a different, luscious, and unique-to-Ample Hills flavor.

Address 305 Nevins Street, Brooklyn, NY 11215, +1 (347)725-4061, www.amplehills.com | Getting there Subway to Union Street (Line R), or bus B 37 to Third Avenue/Union Street | Hours Sun–Thu noon–11pm, Fri & Sat noon–midnight | Tip Just half a mile away are some of the tastiest pies in Brooklyn at Four & Twenty Blackbirds. Order a slice or an entire pie (439 Third Avenue, Brooklyn, NY 11215, www.birdsblack.com).

7 __ Aretsky's Patroon
Casual rooftop bar atop a clubby, ritzy restaurant

In Manhattan's Midtown East, nestled mid-block, lies a hidden gem. Aretsky's Patroon, built in the style of an updated New York City townhouse, was designed as a tri-level steak restaurant. It continues to offer an elegant American Nouveau menu, a posh, clubby atmosphere, and a dazzling personal art photography collection.

Built in the 1950s when modern style was the rage, Aretsky's Patroon is a wider, lighter, 20th-century version of New York's typical late 19th-century brownstones. The owner, Ken Aretsky, formerly of the exclusive 21 Club, is on hand and very hands-on, welcoming his regular customers, many of whom are titans of business and world diplomacy, as many world headquarters and the United Nations are located nearby.

The traditional ground-floor dining room, usually filled to capacity for hushed business lunches, and the myriad posh private second-floor meeting rooms belie the relaxed vibe of the third-floor rooftop bar at Patroon. All summer, the third floor is open-air with hanging planters and lush greenery. In contrast to the formality of the first two floors, the roof is casual with red cushioned benches smartened up with black-and-white striped pillows, wooden high-top and low cocktail tables, festive string lights, and a long, inviting bar sporting wooden bar stools. Sliders, snacks, and fries are on the bar menu all day long, but during lunch, the same excellent à la carte menu served to the swells downstairs is also available on the rooftop.

Cigars are sold and smoked on Patroon's roof, which is open Monday through Friday but closed on weekends when the business-centric neighborhood quiets down. Last call is relatively early, just around 10pm, and the rooftop usually closes by 11pm. In late fall, glass panels are installed, and warm air is piped in, keeping this dapper rooftop bar comfortable and inviting throughout every season.

Address 160 East 46th Street, New York, NY 10017, +1 (212)883-7373, www.aretskyspatroon.com | Getting there Subway to Grand Central–42nd Street (Line 4, 5, 7, S), exit at Lexington Avenue & 42nd Street NW corner, or bus M 102, M 103 to Third Avenue/East 45th Street | Hours Daily 4–10pm | Tip Nearby is Nat Sherman Townhouse, New York City's elegant and expert cigar shop and tobacconist (12 East 42nd Street, New York, NY 10017, www.natsherman.com).

8 Arlo Roof Top (A.R.T.)

An unpretentious oasis in downtown Manhattan

Chef Harold Moore of Harold's Meat + Three serves Southern-inspired comfort food downstairs at Arlo SoHo. Chef Harold also created the rooftop bar, but with a completely different menu inspired by the summery cocktails served on the 11th-floor open-air space called A.R.T. (Arlo Roof Top). To complement your *frosé* (a slushy-style sweet frozen rosé), you might order guacamole and chips or a Mediterranean hummus plate, dishes that are perfectly suited to share with friends on a sultry New York City summer evening.

Another perfect pairing at A.R.T. is the stylish patio furniture with Lower Manhattan vistas, including the Canal Street triangle below. From this 11th-floor aerie above TriBeCa, west of SoHo and south of the West Village, you are high enough above the fray but low enough to feel like part of this rapidly gentrifying neighborhood, newly minted as Hudson Square.

No waiting behind a velvet rope and no reservations make A.R.T. an approachable oasis. When the roof deck gets crowded, or when it's too cold or hot outside, the attached, indoor, year-round bar offers shelter from the elements. There is little shade outside, so wear your best floppy hat and most stylish sunglasses, as you will definitely have a chance to show them off, especially if you arrive before the sun goes down.

Hotel guests frequent the rooftop bar, but the repeat clientele includes creative and entrepreneurial business types who work and live in the neighborhood. Part of Arlo SoHo's overall theme is to create approachable public spaces, so even in the sprawling ground-floor lobby, you'll see lots of people accessing free WiFi as they work on laptops or buying sweets at New York City's only 24-hour Dylan's Candy Bar. But don't let the welcoming lobby distract you from reaching Arlo Roof Top, with its views, vibe, and thoughtful bar and food menus.

Address Arlo SoHo, 231 Hudson Street, 11th Floor, New York, NY 10013, +1 (646)518-8882, www.arlohotels.com/arlo-soho/eat-and-drink/arlo-roof-top, hello@arlohotels.com | **Getting there** Subway to Canal Street (Line 1, A, C, E), or bus M21 to Spring Street/Hudson Street | **Hours** Mon–Thu 4pm–midnight, Fri 4pm–2am, Sat noon–2am, Sun noon–midnight | **Tip** After A.R.T. closes, head around the corner to Ear Inn, a local hangout that's been serving alcohol continuously since 1817. Open daily until 4am with free late-night live music sets three nights a week (326 Spring Street, New York, NY 10013, www.earinn.com).

9 Arthur Ross Terrace

Splash in this playful roof-terrace fountain

While summertime fun in Central Park, the Upper West Side museums, and the shops along Broadway and Columbus is endlessly entertaining, it can get awfully hot and sticky. When a cool-down is in order, take off your shoes and join the kids in the fountain that invites you to walk through it. Lovely to look at, the cool and refreshing water shooting randomly from 2 to 20 feet into the air is even more fun to play in.

What was once an outdoor parking lot is now underground and covered by this one-acre rooftop terrace, whose spectacular centerpiece is the interactive fountain. Intended as a relaxation zone that does not allow radios, skates, scooters, soliciting, or dogs, the Arthur Ross Terrace does indeed encourage the delighted squeals of children running through the fountain's water jets. Designed by Kathryn Gustafson, the terrace's features represent the shadows cast by a lunar eclipse.

The terrace also has café-style seating, shaded benches, shrubbery, and the dramatic backdrop of a giant sphere surrounded by scaffolding and encased in a glass cube that is the Rose Center for Earth & Space at one of New York City's favorite haunts, the American Museum of Natural History.

But it is the accessibility of the fountain that sets it apart. Children are welcome to walk through it, to roll in its gently flowing, watery carpet. They can jump through the four gushing water jets and dump buckets of water on one another's heads. Adults too can cool off by wading barefoot or even lying down and letting water flow around them.

The fountain, as the centerpiece of the terrace, is flat, very shallow and inlaid with lights and tiny mirrors, with designs inspired by the moon and the stars. This acre-sized haven is accessible both from the museum (where there's an admission charge) and from Theodore Roosevelt Park (which is free), just off Columbus Avenue and West 81st Street.

Address West 81st Street & Columbus Avenue, New York, NY 10024, www.amnh.org |
Getting there Subway to 81st Street–Museum of Natural History (Line B on weekdays
only, C), to 79 Street (Line 1), or bus M7, M11, M79 to Columbus Avenue/West 80th
Street | Hours Daily 10am–5:45pm except Thanksgiving and Christmas Day | Tip See
world-class performances each summer when The Public Theater produces Shakespeare
in the Park at the open-air Delacorte Theater (enter Central Park at West 81st Street,
www.publictheater.org/Free-Shakespeare-in-the-Park).

10___Bar 54

The highest outdoor roof bar in Times Square

"Is this building moving?" is an oft-asked question on the long and narrow outdoor terrace of Bar 54, situated 54 floors above the never-ending hubbub of Times Square. The building is most definitely *not* moving, but being this high up, with only a five-foot see-through glass wall between you and eternity, the near-vertigo sensation can happen to sensitive people. They often simply move to the terrace tables further from the glass parapet wall, and those with a more severe fear of heights might move to the luxurious cocoon of the indoor lounge.

To gain access to the amazingly swift 54-floor elevator ride, check in at the restaurant by the hotel entrance for a Bar 54 card, which allows over-21s access to the elevators that are otherwise reserved for overnight guests of the Hyatt Centric. In the warmer months, the terrace is furnished with tables and chairs set under very firmly tethered sail cloth that provides shade to seat 120 comfortably. In the winter, a plastic, temperature-controlled igloo that seats 10 guests is tethered to the terrace for an unusual winter rooftop bar experience. The igloo's sealed entrance from inside ensures guests will not get chilled, even on the most bitter February nights, and the clear plastic allows for iconic views of the Chrysler Building, the Paramount Building, the New Year's Eve crystal ball, and even slivers of both the East and Hudson Rivers.

While reservations are recommended, the terrace seats in *plein air*-summer and in igloo-winter are taken on a first-come-first-served basis. There is no minimum or cover charge, but be warned: the handmade, fresh-ingredient, seasonal cocktails that cannot be replicated start at $26 each. Background music is kept in the background on weekdays and turned up a bit on the weekends for a party atmosphere in the Bar 54 stratosphere. So even if you've promised yourself to avoid the crowds in Times Square, you'll want to make an exception and enjoy it from above.

Address Hyatt Times Square, 135 West 45th, 54th Floor, New York, NY 10036, +1 (646)640-3739, www.hyatt.com/en-US/hotel/new-york/hyatt-centric-times-square-new-york/nycts | Getting there Subway to Times Square–42nd Street (Line 1, 2, 3, N, Q, R, W), to 42nd Street–Port Authority Bus Terminal (Line A, C, E), to Grand Central–42nd Street (Line 4, 5, 6, 7, S), or bus M 5, M 7 to 6th Avenue/West 45th Street | Hours Sun–Wed 4pm–1am, Thu–Sat 4pm–2am | Tip For running enthusiasts, the New York Road Runners' Run Center is the place to go for information about running routes, upcoming races, and even coaching and training classes, as well as a secret New Balance store inside (320 West 57th Street, New York, NY 10019, www.nyrr.org/nyrr-runcenter-featuring-the-new-balance-run-hub).

11_Bar Hugo

What's a bar like you doing in a place like this?

Bar Hugo is not on top of the subway or near hip restaurants and bars or trendy shops. It's not really in SoHo, though it's been called "SoHo East." Two streets away from the Hudson River on an industrial stretch of Greenwich Street, near the Department of Sanitation's truck washing depot and salt shed, and close by a huge UPS distribution center, lies the recently constructed Hotel Hugo, designed by Italian architect Marcello Pozzi. On the hotel's 20th floor is the beautifully appointed Bar Hugo.

Apparently, the fashionistas have discovered Bar Hugo, as it is near Skylight Clarkson Square, an enormous event space that is used for many things, including New York City Fashion Week events each spring and fall. And once a few supermodels have partied at a roof bar, others follow – even if it is slightly off the beaten track.

Bar Hugo rewards you for going out of your way to find it with tasteful original artwork, comfy leather couches, blown glass lighting, and a generous happy hour every Monday through Thursday from 5 to 8pm. Come for the luxury digs and premium cocktails, but stay for the floor-to-ceiling windows that overlook the twinkling city lights on one side of the bar, and the setting sun shimmering over the Hudson River on the other.

This year-round destination with a smart-casual dress code has a large indoor area that will keep you toasty all winter, as well as a narrow West-facing terrace where you can catch the breeze in the warmer months.

Bar Hugo is a dancing destination as well. Shake your booty every Tuesday night at Decades Night, where the DJ spins top hits from the 70s, 80s, and 90s, and flashback cocktails are served, including Kamikazes, Sex on the Beach, and Disco Champagne. Each Sunday, swivel your hips to live Cuban music while sipping cocktails inspired by the Caribbean culture, including classic mojitos.

Address Hotel Hugo, 525 Greenwich Street, 20th Floor, New York, NY 10013, +1 (212)608-4848, www.hotelhugony.com/food-and-drink/bar-hugo-rooftop, reservations@hotelhugony.com | **Getting there** Subway to Houston Street (Line 1, 2), or Spring Street (Line E) | **Hours** Sun–Wed 5–11pm, Thu–Sat 5pm–midnight | **Tip** In the warmer months, party one level up from Bar Hugo at the outdoor Cuban-themed terrace bar Azul on the Rooftop, where it's as if a small slice of Havana landed in Lower Manhattan. The Sunday night Cuban dance party from Bar Hugo moves upstairs and outdoors to Azul during the warmer months (525 Greenwich Street, New York, NY 10013, www.azulrooftop.com).

12   Bar SixtyFive

A bird's nest at the Rainbow Room

In 1934, when the art deco masterpiece Rockefeller Center was completed, Tony Bennett, born in 1926, was merely a lad of eight and had not yet begun his 70-plus-year singing career. Subsequent to recording a successful album with Lady Gaga, 60 years Bennett's junior, she joined him to celebrate his 90th birthday at Radio City Music Hall, the elegant venue built into the ground level of Rockefeller Center. After the show, the party continued with Stevie Wonder, Leslie Odum, Jr., and more top-flight stars, 65 floors up at Bar SixtyFive, where Manhattan's highest and most elegant public-access outdoor rooftop dining and drinking occurs. Just an elevator ride above NBC, the *Saturday Night Live* crew, news anchors, and other TV celebs frequent Bar SixtyFive.

Redesigned with an open-air terrace, Bar SixtyFive is easy to find, as it's just down the hall, black terrazzo with brass inlay, from the landmarked Rainbow Room. Perfectly magical views await you from this airy bird's nest every evening from Sunday through Friday: the vastness of Central Park, sunsets over the Hudson River, and a bird's-eye view of another Manhattan art deco treasure, the Empire State Building.

The room exudes a spare elegance with lots of natural light streaming through the floor-to-ceiling windows to take best advantage of the breathtaking twilight and nighttime views. The sculptural silver ceiling is a contemporary nod to art deco, harmonizing with the room's muted color scheme. Bar SixtyFive's menu features wines, cheeses, and charcuterie, seasonal veggies, meats, and fish, all produced in New York State.

You might not get to sing with Lady Gaga on your birthday, but if you want to celebrate any occasion in high Manhattan style, or just want to turn an ordinary day into an evening to remember, reserve your table at this timeless destination for New York City sophistication since 1934.

Address Rockefeller Center, 30 Rockefeller Plaza, 65th Floor, New York, NY 10112, +1 (212)632-5000, www.rainbowroom.com/bar-sixty-five | Getting there Subway to 47th-50th Streets – Rockefeller Center (Line B, D, F, M weekdays), or bus M 1, M 4, M 50 to West 49th Street / Fifth Avenue | Hours Mon – Fri 5pm – midnight, Sun 4 – 9pm | Tip Go on the Radio City Stage Door Tour, a behind-the-scenes tour of the fabled music hall (1260 Sixth Avenue, New York, NY 10020, www.msg.com/venue-tours/radio-city-music-hall), or The Tour at NBC Studios (The Shop at NBC Studios, 30 Rockefeller Plaza, New York, NY 10112, www.thetouratnbcstudios.com).

13_Barclays Center Green Roof

A green roof grows in Brooklyn

Not since the Dodgers left Brooklyn in 1957 has there been a major sports team that called this borough home, until 2012 when the Brooklyn Nets began playing basketball at the brand new Barclays Center. World-famous pop and rock stars also perform in this 19,000-seat arena. Over 200 events are scheduled annually at Barclays Center, a sports and entertainment hub located at the intersection of three historic Brooklyn neighborhoods and served by nine subway lines, as well as the Long Island Railroad.

Soon after the arena opened, plans to add a green roof emerged, and this complex addition was completed in 2016. Here's why it was so complicated: there are no supporting columns inside the original domed roof, meaning that it was not built to support what, after a saturating rain, would be a 3.4-million-pound green roof. After a storm, each sedum tray, designed to absorb rain water, weighs up to 100 pounds. Multiply this by 34,000 trays that cover the three-acre roof, and you get a very heavy load indeed!

The weight of a three-acre living roof would have crashed right through the original dome, so a super structure of steel beams and trusses was added about 10 feet above the original oyster-shaped roof. This may be why Barclays Center is the only professional sports arena in the United States covered entirely by a green roof.

The living roof absorbs nearly 2 million gallons of rain water annually that would otherwise have overloaded the aging sewer system. The roof also insulates the building, soundproofing it and keeping it cooler in the summer and warmer in the winter. In spring, the roof, a verdant hillside, becomes a flowering habitat for birds and bees. Finally, it makes the arena's weathering steel exterior more attractive from street level, and especially from the surrounding buildings.

Address 620 Atlantic Avenue, Brooklyn, NY 11217, +1 (917)688-6100, www.barclayscenter.com | **Getting there** Subway to Atlantic Avenue – Barclays Center (Line 2, 3, 4, 5, B, D, N, Q, R), bus B 41, B 65 to Flatbush Avenue / Dean Street, or bus B 67 to Flatbush Avenue / Fifth Avenue | **Hours** Unrestricted from street level | **Tip** Catch a performance at the Brooklyn Academy of Music (BAM), a multi-arts center with three theaters, an art-house cinema, and more avant-garde programming at the BAMcafé (30 Lafayette Avenue, Brooklyn, NY 11217, www.bam.org).

14__Bia

Party with a North Vietnamese twist

Bia is a bar, and it's also an eatery serving Northern Vietnamese food made from family recipes handed down for generations. Bia, which means "beer" in Vietnamese, is a gritty neighborhood venue in South Williamsburg built in what was, for decades, a two-bay car repair garage. A long bar dominates the interior where the original brick walls and 17-foot-tall, open-beam ceilings are exposed. As there is no basement underneath Bia to hide the kitchen, the clear pho and other specialty dishes are cooked adjacent to the bar in the kitchen that was added when the garage-turned-restaurant/bar was established.

The single flight of stairs to the rooftop is adorned with murals that continue on the roof as giant portraits, all created by Brooklyn artists. Yet the most obvious feature of Bia's roof is its proximity to the Williamsburg Bridge, suspended just overhead. The trucks and trains rumbling by give Bia's rooftop a distinctly urban look, feel, and sound.

This super casual rooftop seems to be almost an afterthought, with a small standing bar, some mismatched chairs and tables, and a few planters showing off a little greenery. The vine that starts in Bia's backyard has been trained up to the rooftop and sprawls over much of this unmanicured outdoor space. After a long process, Bia has been given permission to serve food as well as drinks on the rooftop starting in 2019.

Loudspeakers hang indoors at Bia from the 17-foot ceiling, pumping up the noise level. But as the owners employ a good neighbor policy, the rooftop broadcasts no music so it is the right setting to meet if you want to have a conversation.

Home-style Northern Vietnamese food, three choices of bottled Vietnamese beers, cocktails, locally-sourced art, friendly staff, and a Rapunzel-like vine on this no-frills rooftop makes Bia the place to kick back with friends on a warm summer's evening.

Address 67 South 6th Street, Brooklyn, NY 11211, +1 (718)388-0908, www.bia.city | **Getting there** Subway to Marcy Avenue (Line J, M), or bus B32, Q59 to Wythe Avenue/South 5th Street | **Hours** Mon–Fri 5pm–4am, Sat & Sun noon–4am | **Tip** Carnivores delight at Peter Luger Steak House, a cash-only joint with a Michelin Star where old-school waiters have served dry-aged beef in a German beer hall setting for over a century (178 Broadway, Brooklyn, NY 11211, www.peterluger.com).

15 _ Blue Ribbon Hi-Bar
A bit of the Hawaiian Islands on Manhattan Island

In Gotham's ever-changing urban restaurant scene, places can come and go in a blink, but somehow, since 1992, Blue Ribbon Sushi has maintained its reputation as the go-to place for consistently excellent sushi throughout Manhattan. But only one of its restaurants serves you a top-notch, full Blue Ribbon dinner menu 14 floors above Columbus Circle in an open-air Hawaiian lanai-inspired rooftop bar.

Blue Ribbon Hi-Bar is a quiet, hidden-away sort of rooftop bar that makes you feel as if you're hanging out at your friend's welcoming and comfortable terrace – that is, if your friend happens to have a double-sided terrace that overlooks Central Park on one side and a famous Sir Norman Foster building on the other.

Up here above Midtown, the mood is relaxed. A fully stocked bar with a low-key bartender in attendance offers cocktails, wine, and an enticing selection of beers. The background music is not at all intrusive, and the orange walls and large floral cushions evoke an island setting – not so much the island of Manhattan, but rather the trade winds of the Hawaiian Islands.

Patrons of the Blue Ribbon Sushi Bar & Grill downstairs might come up for a drink and one of the expertly made sushi rolls while they are waiting for their downstairs table, or they might be seduced by the open-air, laid-back atmosphere and casual string filament lighting at Hi-Bar, and decide to order their full meal to be served up here.

In cooler months, the retractable roof is shuttered, but there is always a small open-air terrace behind the bar for a peek into Columbus Circle and Central Park. However, when it's warm and comfortable out, and you don't have time to travel thousands of miles by jet to get to Hawaii's Big Island, consider instead a much more pleasant journey to the penthouse of the Sixty Hotel in Columbus Circle for an evening at Blue Ribbon Hi-Bar.

Address 6 Columbus Hotel, 308 West 58th Street, 14th Floor, New York, NY 10019, +1 (212)397-0404, www.blueribbonrestaurants.com/restaurants/blue-ribbon-hi-bar | Getting there Subway to 59th Street–Columbus Circle (Line 1, A, B, C, D), or bus M5, M7, M10, M20, M104 to Columbus Circle/8th Avenue | Hours Daily 5pm–midnight | Tip What the Wall Street Journal calls "easily the most high-end museum gift shop in the country," The Store at MAD is across the street at the entrance to the Museum of Arts & Design. Shop for limited edition glass, ceramics, housewares, jewelry, and more (2 Columbus Circle, New York, NY 10019, www.thestore.madmuseum.org).

16_ Boardwalk & Vine

For a vacation view, turn right on the boardwalk

Today, the best way to get to Coney Island is via subway, which drops you an easy block from the beach. Most people turn *left* at the boardwalk, drawn that way by amusements, rides, ice cream, and changing rooms next to the beach. Next time, turn *right*, and you will be richly rewarded at Kitchen 21's landmark rooftop, Boardwalk & Vine.

Nearly a century ago, during Coney Island's heyday, frequent ferries transported streams of mostly middle-class people to Steeplechase Pier. The bustling Coney Island boardwalk was then dotted with numerous palaces, lavishly decorated with hand-painted, nautical-themed detailing: a grand bathhouse, a seaside hotel, and Childs Restaurant's flagship location.

Childs was a chain of moderately priced, cafeteria-style eateries. The Coney Island boardwalk location was their showplace, a cavernous restaurant with high ceilings, enormous ocean-facing windows, and an accessible rooftop where patrons could gaze across the sea. Childs' intricate and elegant ocean-themed decorations included arches and finials of seashells, snails, octopi, lobsters, crabs, fish, seahorses, and scallops. Guests felt they had arrived somewhere very special indeed.

As the Great Depression took its toll on Coney Island, the boardwalk palaces were torn down, except for Childs, which fell into disrepair until 2002, when it was recognized as a New York City landmark. Today, the terracotta detail has been painstakingly restored, and the building houses Kitchen 21, a restaurant with a spacious, airy rooftop bar called Boardwalk & Vine. Up here, overlooking the beach and boardwalk, guests are near enough to inspect the lovely details up close.

The roof is perfect for watching summer Friday night fireworks and the iconic Parachute Jump tower. It's easy to take the subway to your next beach vacation – just remember to turn *right* to Boardwalk & Vine!

Address 3052 West 21st Street, Brooklyn, NY 11224, +1 (718)996-0502, www.kitchen-21.com |
Getting there Subway to Coney Island–Stillwell Avenue (Line D, F, N, Q), or bus B 36 to Surf
Avenue/West 21st Street | Hours Fri–Sun 3–11pm | Tip Take in a concert, family show,
sporting event, comedy, or multicultural event at the outdoor 5,000-seat Ford Amphitheater
at Coney Island Boardwalk, adjacent to Boardwalk & Vine (3052 West 21st street, Brooklyn,
NY 11224, www.fordamphitheaterconeyisland.com).

17   Bookmarks

A sky-high toast to literature

This "silver building," just 25 feet wide and 100 feet long, was built in 1912, one year before the neighboring Grand Central Terminal was completed. Before functioning as a book-lovers hotel, 299 Madison has served many purposes in its 100-plus years of existence. One notable regular was Theodore Roosevelt, the rough riding, beloved 26th president of the United States, and a New York City native. "Teddy" (after whom the teddy bear was named) kept an office in this building after he left office and worked as a contributing editor to *The Outlook*, a news and editorial magazine.

In 1912, a well-designed building often had an outdoor roof terrace for entertaining or simply fresh air, and this fashionable neo-Gothic style building is no exception. Although Bookmarks is a multi-room rooftop bar and lounge, the small outdoor area that seats around 50 people is much more reminiscent of a wealthy New Yorker's private terrace than a bar. Try the cleverly named cocktails, such as the Tequila Mockingbird (Sauza Blue tequila, agave nectar, fresh lime juice, minced ginger), the F. Scotch Fitzergald (brown buttered Glenmorangie 10 Year scotch, Campari, Carpano AnticaIt), or the Pullitzer (Dorothy Parker gin, St. Germain, Fernet Branca, agave nectar).

Get to Bookmarks early in summertime, as the outdoor space is the first area to fill up. Otherwise, there are two glassed-in solariums aptly named The Poetry Lounge and The Writer's Den. Inside is a mahogany-hued lounge filled with books and deep cushioned chairs where the busiest place in the bar during colder months is next to the glowing fireplace.

In this Midtown location next to countless corporate offices, Grand Central Terminal, Bryant Park, and the main branch of the New York Public Library, Bookmarks is a timeless neighborhood gem that welcomes a primarily local clientele of all ages.

Address Library Hotel, 299 Madison Avenue, 14th Floor, New York, NY 10017, +1 (212)204-5498, www.hospitalityholdings.com/#/establishments/bookmarks | Getting there Subway to Grand Central–42nd Street (Line 4, 5, 6, 7, S), or bus M1, M2, M3, M4 to Madison Avenue / East 40th Street | Hours Sun–Thu 4pm–midnight, Fri & Sat 4pm–1am | Tip Library Way, along East 41st Street starting at Park Avenue and ending at the grand, lion-flanked entrance of the New York Public Library on Fifth Avenue, features famous literary quotes about reading, writing, and literature emblazoned on 96 bronze plaques embedded in the sidewalk (www.grandcentralpartnership.nyc/our-neighborhood/library-way).

18_Boxers Hell's Kitchen

The gay sports bar we all need

True story: two guys on a gay softball team realized there were no gay-friendly sports bars for after-game drinks, so they opened one! Nearly a decade later, Boxers is a rapidly growing chain of gay sports bars that sponsor dozens of LGBT (Lesbian Gay Bisexual Transgender) leagues throughout New York City: everything from wrestling to SCUBA to cheerleading, and, of course, softball.

If a sports bar that serves food, and has flirtatious, scantily clad bartenders and servers to entertain men sounds familiar, it should. Hooters™, established in 1983, has locations nationwide. Almost 30 years later, a similar concept opened in New York City – but this time the hot-looking servers and bartenders dress in red boxer shorts, and the employees wearing these tiny uniforms are primarily in-shape gay men.

Boxers, named after the ubiquitous red shorts, also uses the Boxer dog breed as its mascot. Though all are welcome, and it's not unusual to see groups of women or mixed-gender corporate events, the Boxers concept is a gay sports bar. Boxers Hell's Kitchen is the burgeoning company's largest and busiest venue with three floors, and the only one with a rooftop bar and restaurant.

Manhattan has frequent spring, summer, and fall bouts of rain, but the open-air rooftop is partially covered, so until it gets cold enough to freeze the soda gun pipes, Boxers Hell's Kitchen keeps the rooftop open to guests. It's busiest on warm summer nights, and during the popular Sunday brunch seatings between noon and 4pm. Though the rooftop has plenty of tables, no advance reservations are taken; arrive early to stake out your spot.

Friendly service and customer contentment are emphasized at Boxers Hell's Kitchen so try a unique drink or something new on the large menu because your handsome, friendly server will make sure you like it, or replace it with something you will like.

Address 742 Ninth Avenue, New York, NY 10019, +1 (212)951-1518, www.boxersnyc.com | **Getting there** Subway to 50th Street (Line C, E), or bus M 11 to 9th Avenue / West 50th Street | **Hours** Mon – Thu 4pm – 2am, Fri 4pm – 4am, Sat noon – 4am, Sun noon – 2am, Sun brunch noon – 4pm | **Tip** Across the street, The Sound Bite Restaurant offers live jazz and blues sets, along with award-winning blackened hot wings from a menu filled with Cajun, Southern, and Italian fusion food (737 Ninth Avenue, New York, NY 10019, +1 (917)409-5868, www.thesoundbiterestaurant.com).

19 Brass Monkey

The old Meatpacking District we knew and loved

The Meatpacking District, once the epicenter of New York's butchering industry, is now a huge destination for New York's famous night life. Streams of people dressed in their highest heels or newest silk shirt expect to wait in line behind the red velvet ropes, hoping to be admitted to a snazzy lounge or trendy club. Brass Monkey's casual rooftop is the welcome antidote to all that.

In 2008, a few years after smoking in bars became illegal, the Brass Monkey proprietors opened their unused rooftop space, mainly to offer patrons a place to light up. Much to their surprise, but to nobody else's, the roof is where everyone wanted to be, mostly in warm weather, but even on cooler nights.

Ten years later, the Brass Monkey's rooftop bar has doubled in size and is a non-smoking, non-stop party deck all summer long. Handsome sailcloth shades offer some protection from the sun. The hanging herb garden on the back wall is flourishing. When harvested, these roof-grown herbs enhance the Brass Monkey's handmade cocktails. The beer list is extensive and popular with the unpretentious crowd. Listen to the music and happy chatter in this welcoming day-and-night establishment. As it's a great place to unwind with friends and stay a while, the good news is that the hearty and delicious food is also served on the rooftop.

The Brass Monkey has no vista to boast about, but it has a very unusual view. This third-floor roof deck is adjacent to the concrete stilts that support the towering Standard Hotel, turning the cozy Brass Monkey into a bit of a flannel-shirted David next to a fashion-conscious Goliath.

Rooftop drinking and eating starts at 11am every day during the summer season. Seeking a mellower rooftop experience? Try Brass Monkey during weekday lunchtimes. Looking for a welcoming, raucous party atmosphere? Check it out all weekend long, day or night.

Address 55 Little West 12th Street, New York, NY 10014, +1 (844)344-1200, www.brassmonkeynyc.com | Getting there Subway to 14th Street (Line A, C, E), to 14th Street (Line 2, 3), or bus M 11, M 12, M 14D to West 14th Street/Washington Street | Hours Daily 11am–4am (rooftop closes a little earlier at management's discretion) | Tip The Golf Club at Chelsea Piers has a unique multilevel driving range to perfect your swing (59 Chelsea Piers, New York, NY 10011, www.chelseapiers.com/Golf).

20__Broken Shaker New York
A Caribbean island in the New York City skyline

This story starts in Miami, not New York City, around a swimming pool and not on a rooftop. Two friends who love to invent cocktails and who believe that drinking should be fun created a Caribbean-chic pop-up bar around the pool at the Miami Freehand Hotel. Called Broken Shaker, it was planned to be open for a month in 2012. The bar was such a hit that the pop-up evolved into permanent partnership with the Sydell Group, giving Broken Shaker a home in all four Freehand hotels: Miami and Chicago at street level, and Los Angeles and New York on rooftops.

Broken Shaker does not 1) require reservations, 2) have bottle service, or 3) demand that you wait behind a velvet rope. It does have friendly bar and wait staff, plants and colors galore, lots of cozy rooftop nooks, and 360-degree city views. It has three cocktail menus: one specific to New York City, another to Miami, and a third with the most popular drinks from LA and Chicago. So your challenge is choosing among all the boozy options. For a nosh to accompany your Poppyseed Bagel Fizz, one of the New York cocktails, the menu is filled with Middle Eastern and Caribbean flavors, plus a beloved American original, soft serve vanilla ice cream dipped in chocolate.

This bohemian getaway has a vintage sound system with an eclectic playlist that adds even more color to the saturated hues, and thrift-shop-found treasures that make Broken Shaker feel like your coolest friend's roof terrace. Adding to its hidden urban aesthetic, an old freight elevator ferries guests up to the 18th floor six at a time. And just maybe it feels like your hip friend's terrace because one of the owners, Elad Zvi, started out washing dishes at the Plaza Hotel and worked his way up the food and beverage chain until he and his partner, Gabriel Orta, were able to create their own place to have fun in the New York City skyline.

Address 23 Lexington Avenue, 18th Floor, New York, NY 10010, +1 (212)475-1920, www.freehandhotels.com/new-york/broken-shaker | **Getting there** Subway to 23rd Street (Line 6), or bus M 102, M 103 to East 24th Street / Lexington Avenue | **Hours** Daily 4pm – 2am | **Tip** Missing an exotic recipe ingredient? For a vast array of Indian and Middle Eastern spices, plus so many global foods it boggles the mind, visit Kalustyan's (123 Lexington Avenue, New York, NY 10016, www.foodsofnations.com).

21 Bronx County Courthouse

Making the case for living roofs

Hidden on top of the elegant, classical revival style Bronx County Courthouse is a little-known jewel tucked behind a 10-foot parapet wall: a 10,000-square-foot green roof. The limestone and granite courthouse was completed in 1934, added to the National Register of Historical Places in 1983, and crowned with the first "extensive" (meaning that plants are grown in four inches of soil) green roof in the South Bronx in 2006. This was also the first green roof on any of the 53 New York City Department of Citywide Administration Services buildings.

As this building is a functioning courthouse for the New York State Supreme Court of Bronx County, visitors are required to call in advance to schedule a viewing, plus submit to an extensive security check before being permitted to enter. But it's worth the effort. And be aware that while you may enter with your cell phone, even if it has a camera feature, standard cameras are not allowed.

Once inside, take the elevator to the ninth floor and follow the signs to the green roof. You will be walking past courthouse employees' offices during business hours, so please show proper courtesy. Step through the unassuming door to discover the courthouse's living treasure.

The roof was planted primarily with multiple varieties of flowering sedum in shallow, lightweight soil, but the designer added deeper growing medium across the length of this rectangular green roof in the shape of a dramatic wave, where tall meadow grasses reach several feet in height. You'll also see electronic equipment in the midst of the green roof, collecting scientific data to quantify the roof's benefits, such as storm water absorption and cooler roof temperatures. The parapet wall surrounding the green roof protects the plants from wind, but it unfortunately blocks what would be clear views of the Grand Concourse, Yankee Stadium, and Manhattan.

Address 851 Grand Concourse, Bronx, NY 10451, +1 (718)590-3545 | Getting there Subway to 161st Street – Yankee Stadium (Line 4, B, D), or bus Bx 1, Bx 2 to Grand Concourse / East 161st Street | Hours Mon – Fri 9am – 4pm, reservations required | Tip Visit four Depression-era murals in the spectacular rotunda on the ground floor of the Courthouse that depict the history of the Bronx, including the arrival of Jonas Bronck, after whom the borough is named, and who purchased the land from the local Native American Lenape people.

22 Bronx Library Center Outdoor Reading Terrace

Get your daily dose of news and vitamin D

Everyone knows libraries are where books can be borrowed free of charge, but books are just the beginning of your visit to the Bronx Library Center. This modern, inviting, and sunlight-filled branch of the New York Public Library is a state-of-the-art knowledge resource for the multicultural Bronx community and happens to have what no other library in New York City has: an outdoor reading terrace open to all.

The third floor is home to the Bronx's largest collection of circulating books, as well as magazines and newspapers. Grab a copy of today's *New York Times*, the latest from your favorite author, or whatever else grabs your imagination, and take it outside to read for a while. Enjoy some fresh air and sunshine while updating yourself on whatever delights you.

Large and 'green,' this six-story building that opened in 2006 was awarded a coveted LEED™ Silver certificate. Popular books and DVDs are available on the first floor. Story time and family literacy workshops are found in the children's area on the second floor. Computers and laptops with internet access are available throughout the building. A large, comfortable auditorium for film screenings, exhibitions, job fairs, and live music performances is downstairs. Adult classes to improve speaking and reading English are offered. Computer training, career coaching, and job search help is also available. After-school educational programs and intensive college readiness programs are available for teens. Explore the excellent in-house collection of rare Spanish/English materials reflecting the Latino experience. You can even get your New York ID card at this library branch. Amazingly, all of this, plus your daily dose of sunshine, is available completely free of charge.

Address 310 East Kingsbridge Road, Bronx, NY 10458, +1 (718)579-4244, www.nypl.org/blc | **Getting there** Subway to Kingsbridge Road (Line D), or bus Bx 9 to East Kingsbridge Road / East 192nd Street | **Hours** Mon–Sat 9am–9pm, Sun noon–6pm | **Tip** Gain insight into the pastoral and literary past of the Bronx with a visit to the final home of author and poet Edgar Allan Poe. His wife Virginia died of tuberculosis in the first-floor bedroom here in 1847 (2640 Grand Concourse, Bronx, NY 10458, www.bronxhistoricalsociety.org/poe-cottage).

23___Brooklyn Banya Rooftop

Roll around in the snow – in your bathing suit

Let's make this perfectly clear: Brooklyn Banya is not a spa. It's not modern, refined, or even peaceful during its busiest hours. It is, rather, a Russian bathhouse – social, casual, family friendly, and unpretentious. Besides the indoor pool and hot tub, there are three hot rooms with varying levels of humidity: the 200-degree Russian dry sauna heated by tons of river rocks, the wet and dry Turkish-style sauna where guests can pour buckets of cold water over their heads to cool down, and the more modern steam room with air so thick it's like sitting in a cloud.

A café sells pickle plates and borscht, as well as wine and beer. Bathers of legal age can bring their own vodka to complete the Russian experience.

Year round, Brooklyn Banya encourages people to enjoy their clean and unfussy facilities to sweat out toxins and reinvigorate their immune systems, as Russian people from all strata of society have been doing for centuries. Some say a few hours at Brooklyn Banya having a good *shvitz* (sweat) is equivalent to a 21-day detox diet.

Above this old-world, holistic health destination is an easily accessible rooftop. There are lounge chairs, potted plants, and a dish of kibble for the Banya's resident cat who has free reign throughout the 10,000-square-foot baths. During summer, guests sun themselves, nap between saunas, and gossip with friends. However, the most popular time on the rooftop is just after a brisk snowfall. In one of the most unique uses of a New York City rooftop, overheated bathers dash up the stairs to roll around in the fresh snow.

The first Russian bathhouse in the world to be owned by a single woman, Brooklyn Banya's mission since 1996 has been to welcome all who want to experience an old and enjoyable way to stay healthy and vigorous. And what could be more fun than rolling around on a rooftop in fresh snow – in your swimsuit?

Address 602 Coney Island Avenue, Brooklyn, NY 11218, +1 (718)853-1300, www.brooklynbanya.com | Getting there Subway to Beverley Road (Line Q), or bus B 68 to Coney Island Avenue/Slocum Place | Hours Mon–Fri 11am–11pm, Sat & Sun 8am–11pm | Tip A short walk from the Banya is Kensington Stables. Go on a 3.5-mile horseback ride along the bridle path in Prospect Park, or sign up for regular lessons (51 Caton Place, Brooklyn, NY 11218, www.kensingtonstables.com).

24 Brooklyn Botanic Garden
Where bees and butterflies are your hosts

Until 1898, all five boroughs of New York City were independent municipalities. Naturally, there has been competition among the boroughs, especially the two wealthiest and most populated ones, Manhattan and Brooklyn. Both proudly boast world-class performing arts venues, magnificent art museums, impressive libraries, and grand city parks designed by Olmsted & Vaux. But in 1910, Brooklyn's philanthropists created a public institution that Manhattan has never had: the 52-acre Brooklyn Botanic Garden (BBG). More than 100 years later, BBG continues to be a major attraction, with over 700,000 visitors annually and numerous mature and multifaceted gardens throughout.

As the institution passed its centennial, as part of their *Campaign for the Next Century*, BBG opened a state-of-the-art Visitor Center topped with 40,000 plants on its leaf-shaped living roof.

The 9,400-square-foot, curvilinear roof meadow atop the new Visitor Center is a complex canvas planted with native flowering plants, bulbs, and grasses designed to display seasonal changes in color and texture. It's no surprise that the BBG Visitor Center won a New York City Design Commission Award for Design Excellence. The semi-intensive (meaning the plants are in about eight inches of soil) green roof's runoff flows into a daisy-chain series of rain gardens that conserve 200,000 gallons of water annually. The living roof insulates the Visitor Center below it and reduces storm water overflow by acting like a giant sponge.

Designed to attract hummingbirds, butterflies, and pollinating bees, the roof has also hosted some surprise visitors. A gardener recently reported a duck nest with 6 eggs hidden in the tall grasses. Get the best view of this ever-changing, eco-forward living roof from the benches on the Overlook located behind the Visitors Center, amongst the garden's collection of mature ginkgo trees.

Address 900 Washington Avenue, Brooklyn, NY 11255, +1 (718)623-7200, www.bbg.org |
Getting there Subway to Eastern Parkway–Brooklyn Museum (Line 2, 3), to Franklin
Avenue (Line 4, 5), to Prospect Park (Line B), or bus B 41 to Flatbush Avenue / Park
Entrance | Hours See website for seasonal hours | Tip Next door, explore the extensive
collections at the venerable Brooklyn Museum. Keep an eye out for their innovative
exhibitions (200 Eastern Parkway, Brooklyn, NY 11238, www.brooklynmuseum.org).

25 Brooklyn Children's Museum

A new roof on the world's oldest children's museum

In culturally diverse Crown Heights, where rows of late 19th-century homes are red-brick and brownstone, lies an architectural surprise: the very modern Brooklyn Children's Museum. Covered with a million tiny, sunshine-yellow tiles atop giant blocks of red and green, it attracts children like a huge toy magnet. Inside, the museum offers 100,000 square feet of hands-on, experiential exhibits primarily designed for kids aged 0 to 8.

Still in the original location but now in its third iteration, the Brooklyn Children's Museum was founded in 1899 as an annex of the nearby Brooklyn Museum. Originally housed in two large Victorian mansions, it was the first museum designed for children, and it was extremely popular from its inception. In 1967, the mansions were torn down, and the museum was rebuilt underground. After the museum's centennial, architect Rafael Viñoly was hired to design a modern space atop the subterranean structure. He added the primary color block scheme, lots of airy, open exhibit spaces, and a sprawling 20,000-square-foot, easily accessible rooftop.

The roof is large enough for community events that celebrate central Brooklyn's varied cultures, like the annual rooftop *sukkah* for the Jewish high holidays, yet small enough to allow tots the freedom to wander and play in a safe space.

The roof garden's centerpiece is Toshiko Mori's striking structure that provides shelter from rain. Built of curved tubular steel and translucent material stretching between the tubes, it looks like an enormous winged creature has landed. A garden features exclusively native-to-New York plants, including blueberries that the kids can pick and eat, a boardwalk-style path, and easily climbable logs. Adirondack chairs adorn the turf where music events take place.

Address 145 Brooklyn Avenue, Brooklyn, NY 11213, +1 (718)735-4400, www.brooklynkids.org | Getting there Subway to Kingston Avenue (Line 3), to Kingston-Throop Avenue (Line C), or bus B 43, B 65 to Brooklyn Avenue/Bergen Street | Hours Rooftop open during warm weather Tue, Wed & Fri 10am–5pm, Thu 10am–6pm, Sat & Sun 10am–7pm | Tip It's a short walk to the Jewish Children's Museum, "a place of learning and wonder," that is designed for elementary school-aged children from all faiths and backgrounds to learn about Jewish history and heritage (792 Eastern Parkway, Brooklyn, NY 11213, www.jcm.museum).

26 Brooklyn Crab

Statue of Liberty views from a beachy crab shack

Brooklyn Crab has a chilled-out atmosphere you'd expect to find on Montauk, Long Island rather than in Red Hook, Brooklyn. The best description is "beach casual." You'll fit right in wearing your loudest Aloha shirt, board shorts, flip-flops, and sunglasses. Seating is at picnic benches or wooden booths. Your fellow beach bums are having a rousing good time. And the kitchen is working hard to keep up with the orders coming in for buckets of fresh crabs, steamed lobsters, barbequed shrimp, and fresh clams and oysters.

It's a little off the beaten path, so getting to Brooklyn Crab can be a challenge – it's not very close to a subway or bus stop. But there are options. Take the subway and walk a ways, or travel by bus, which will leave you closer. Brooklyn Crab is actually convenient by car, as there is plenty of street parking nearby. Or ride your bike. The most scenic way to get to this kitchy-beachy, tri-level seafood shack, though, is to take one of the two boat services that sail out of Lower Manhattan. The New York City Ferry offers a South Brooklyn-bound ferry boat from the Wall Street/Pier 11 landing. A few blocks north is another water transportation option at South Street Seaport: the Ikea Water Taxi, a yellow boat accented with black-and-white checkers, that ferries shoppers to the giant furniture store in Red Hook, in easy walking distance of Brooklyn Crab.

If you have to wait for the second- or third-floor roof decks, then go play in the backyard! Try your hand at corn hole or pick up a putter for 18 holes of mini-golf. A bar and limited backyard menu will keep you in food and drinks, and hanging out with the ever-changing cast of characters will keep you entertained before being called to an upstairs table, where you can delight in a breezy atmosphere within viewing distance of Lady Liberty and New York Harbor.

Check the website for an array of happenings, including Crabby Hour, Pint Night, and Trivia Mondays.

Address 24 Reed Street, Brooklyn, NY 11231, +1 (718)643-2722, www.brooklyncrab.com | Getting there Subway to Smith–9th Street (Line F, G), or bus B 61 to Beard Street/ Van Brunt Street | Hours Sun–Thu 11:30am–10pm, Fri & Sat 11:30am–11pm | Tip Visit the Waterfront Museum on a big, red, 1914 floating barge, where you will learn about New York's coastal history (free open boat tours Sat 1 – 5pm & Thu 4 – 8pm; 290 Conover Street, Brooklyn, NY 11231, www.waterfrontmuseum.org).

27___Brooklyn Grange

Profitable, responsible, and sustainable roof farms

In 2010, urban farming began looking up – to New York City roof-tops! That year, the entrepreneurs behind Brooklyn Grange created the first-ever, one-acre commercial rooftop farm in Queens. In 2012, the business expanded with the one-and-a-half-acre rooftop farm planted on top of Building 3 at the 150-year-old Brooklyn Navy Yard in Wallabout Bay. In 2018, the third and largest farm was added on a massive three-acre rooftop in Brooklyn's Sunset Park, making their farm about five acres across three rooftop properties.

Most farms, especially those practicing organic principles, can't farm profitably on just five acres, but Brooklyn Grange has built an entire industry on these three rooftops. Other than farming a diz-zying variety of greens, berries, herbs, tomatoes, flowers, peppers, etc., they have taken advantage of the breezy climates and beautiful views, and created a series of rooftop events: everything from yoga to farm dinners to weddings and corporate team-building events. A CSA (community supported agriculture), in which subscribers get a weekly portion of whatever has just been harvested, is offered. The Grange is partnered with a nonprofit that teaches children to farm. They offer rooftop classes, act as urban farming consultants, and lec-ture locally and across the globe. While rooftop farming happens pri-marily between May and October, the busy bees at the Grange (not the ones in the rooftop bee hives, though they have over 300 honey bee hives ensconced on rooftops throughout New York City!) keep buzzing all year long.

Another option to experience the Grange is with a professional tour guide who will take you to several remarkable Brooklyn sites, *including* a stop at the rooftop farm in the Navy Yard. Register in advance for events, classes, dinners, and tours on the Grange's web-site as gaining entry to the security-conscious Brooklyn Navy Yard requires showing the gate guard an invitation.

Address Brooklyn Navy Yard, Building 3, 63 Flushing Avenue, 11th Floor, Brooklyn, NY 11205, +1 (347)670-3660, www.brooklyngrangefarm.com, info@brooklyngrangefarm.com | Getting there Subway to Clinton–Washington Avenues (Line G), to York Street (Line F), both with long walks, bus B 48 to Flushing Avenue/Clinton Avenue, or bus B 57, B 69 to Cumberland Street/Flushing Avenue | Hours May–Oct tours each Wed at 10am & 11:30am with advanced reservation | Tip Brooklyn Grange's Flagship Farm in Long Island City, Queens has a weekly free open house every Saturday between May and October. Meet the farm team (and the chickens) and take home some fresh produce (37-18 Northern Boulevard, Queens, NY 11101, www.brooklyngrangefarm.com).

28 Bushwick Inlet Park

Priceless skyline views free at a Brooklyn rooftop

Just a few minutes' walk from some of the trendiest rooftop bars in Brooklyn is a cutting-edge rooftop park. In 2013, the long-held promise of creating a park along the North Williamsburg waterfront was realized, and its outstanding feature is a living roof that covers the entire building at the entrance of the park.

The perfect place for a sunny, shaded, or starlit bit of relaxation, Bushwick Inlet Park has an earth-sheltered facilities building with a sloping, grass-covered roof that is easily accessible and inviting. It extends the park from the water's edge to the top of this two-story building, making every inch of this 6.2-acre site accessible to the public. The zigzag path along the sloping roof provides ADA (Americans with Disabilities Act) access to the large shaded canopy at the top so everyone can enjoy this park. And it is worth the effort. From this constructed hillside perch, the view extends over the uninterrupted green roof to the grassy playing fields and across the East River to the Manhattan skyline. While the West-facing façade is completely covered with living matter, there is streetside access along Kent Avenue to the attractive building below that houses an active community center as well as park maintenance equipment.

Employing the entire array of environmentally progressive technologies, the facilities building has geothermal wells for efficient heating and cooling, a system to collect rainwater that is later used for irrigating the grassy roof, a solar canopy that provides more than 50% of the building's energy needs, and, of course, the green roof to absorb storm water runoff, usually considered to be a New York City infrastructure conundrum. It's no surprise that this New York City Department of Parks and Recreation building has won numerous awards, including the AIA/COTE Top Ten Green Projects in 2014.

Address 86 Kent Avenue, Brooklyn, NY 11211, www.nycgovparks.org/parks/
bushwickinletpark | Getting there Subway to Bedford Avenue (Line L), 10 minute walk |
Hours Daily 6am–10pm | Tip Visit Smorgasburg, arguably the best food market in the
city. Every weekend, more than 75 local food vendors offer fantastic savory and sweet treats
from around the world served with a unique Brooklyn twist. See their website for locations,
as the market moves seasonally (www.smorgasburg.com).

29 __ The Cantor Roof Garden
Open-air art, drinks, and views at the Met

Imagine being selected to create a site-specific, original work of art for an enormous outdoor exhibit space at one of the world's most beloved museums. It actually happens each year at the Metropolitan Museum of Art, New York City's world-renowned art museum. The Cantor Roof Garden is the 8,000-square-foot rooftop that overlooks the canopy of Central Park's trees. Each year since 1998, just one artist receives this fantastic opportunity.

Past exhibitors include art-world superstars Roy Lichtenstein, Sol LeWitt, Jeff Koons, and Andy Goldsworthy. Some years, such as when the identical twin artists, Doug and Mike Starn, created *Big Bambú*, museum visitors can interact with and even climb through the installations. Sometimes the work is political, and occasionally whimsical, but the exhibit is always original and specific to the roof of the Met.

The Iris and B. Gerald Cantor Roof Garden opens each May and stays open until November during museum hours, including the rooftop's most popular times on Friday and Saturday nights when the Met stays open until 9pm. Soft drinks, cocktails, and light snacks are sold on the roof, making it a popular destination by day and a romantic date spot on sultry summer nights. However, if it rains, even a little bit, the roof becomes off limits. So it's best to check the forecast before you go.

The Cantor Roof Garden is available via one bank of elevators in the southern wing of this vast museum. First-time guests may have to ask how to get to the rooftop, but be assured, it is worth the search. Once you have found your way to the roof, stay a while. Have a drink or a snack, enjoy the panoramic views of Central Park West and Central Park South, the mind-expanding art installation, and the endless communing of art enthusiasts from across the globe. Remember to wear a hat if you're there during the day, as shade can be scarce.

Address 1000 Fifth Avenue, New York, NY 10028, +1 (800)662-3397, www.metmuseum.org | Getting there Subway to 86th Street (Line 4, 5, 6), bus M1, M3, M4 to Fifth Avenue/ East 81st Street, or bus M2 to Fifth Avenue/East 84th Street | Hours Sun–Thu 10am–5:30pm, Fri & Sat 10am–9pm | Tip Older than Central Park, The Arsenal is an historic building resembling a medieval fortress. It has a crenulated cornice, a doorway guarded by a cast-iron eagle, and is home to the Arsenal Gallery (830 Fifth Avenue, New York, NY 10065, www.nycgovparks.org/about/history/the-arsenal).

30__Cary Leeds Center for Tennis & Learning

A world-class tennis center for everyone

Tennis, "the sport of kings," has long been associated with privilege, wealth, and private clubs. However, in 1968, when Arthur Ashe broke the color barrier as the first black man to win the US Open, he made it his personal mission that all children should be able to use tennis, along with education, as a launching pad to future success. As a result of his efforts, nonprofit tennis and education programs have been helping kids for more than four decades.

In 2017, the first New York Junior Tennis & Learning (NYJTL) flagship facility was completed on the edge of Crotona Park in the South Bronx. Within walking distance of 30,000 school-age kids, the Cary Leeds Center for Tennis & Learning is the manifestation of Arthur Ashe's NYJTL dream.

This active community center, educational facility, and pristine tennis center with 20 regulation and two stadium courts also features state-of-the-art classrooms, a gym, and separate locker rooms for adults and children. The elevated viewing deck and roof terrace provide excellent vantage points for viewing the matches.

Adult academies offer intensive training by world-class tennis stars, while children, starting in elementary school, can advance their level of play through expert instruction free of charge. Innovative programs, such as Serve & Connect, pair neighborhood kids and volunteer police officers for 12 weeks of tennis so they can get to know each other as friends.

Cary Leeds hosts the world's best under-18 players for the Junior US Open Qualifying matches. Winners go to the US Open tournament in Flushing, Queens. The Little Mo tournament, where many of today's tennis stars were first noticed, is also hosted here. Kids at Cary Leeds hone their tennis abilities and learn valuable life skills.

Address 1720 Crotona Avenue, Bronx, NY 10457, +1 (718)247-7420, www.nyjtl.org, caryleedsinfo@nyjtl.org | **Getting there** Subway to 174th Street (Line 2, 5), or bus BX 17 to Crotona Avenue / Crotona Park Building | **Hours** Daily 7am – 10pm | **Tip** Crotona Pool, a massive, 330-foot-long public swimming facility, is a six-minute walk away. It's free of charge and open all summer long (1700 Fulton Avenue, Bronx, NY 10457, www.nycgovparks.org/parks/crotona-park/facilities/outdoor-pools/crotona-pool).

31 Castell Rooftop Lounge
Cava towers and martinis with a Spanish twist

Spain has some wild traditions. The world's largest tomato fight occurs each August in Valencia. Every June near Burgos, grown men dressed as the devil leap over babies at the festival of *El Colacho*. In Pamplona each summer, thousands of intoxicated people run alongside sober, angry bulls at the San Fermín festival. Not to be outdone, in Catalonia, there is the centuries-old spectacle of *castell*, building complex human towers up to 10 stories. When a castell is built and deconstructed without a single person falling, it is considered a success, and it is this Spanish tradition after which Castell, a refined New York City rooftop martini lounge, is named.

To honor this tradition, every afternoon at around 4:30, the bar sets up a castell of champagne glasses, and pours cava, Spanish sparkling wine, into the top glass. When the castell is constructed properly, the cava cascades into the tower of glasses without spilling a drop. Once the ritual is complete, the cava is complimentary, and the festive atmosphere comes alive.

During summer, the spacious terrace has black-cushioned banquettes and dramatic chairs that form semi-private nooks. The greenery along the terrace edge and in planters livens up the sophisticated black décor. A standing marble bar is available for when Castell is busiest, usually after weekday working hours.

Terrace views are dramatic in both directions. Looking south, it's like a painting of old New York City with at least seven cedar water towers in plain view. The northern view, dominated by the *New York Times* building, reveals a 52-story Renzo Piano skyscraper that reaches as high as the Chrysler Building.

Castell is also a great winter bar. The indoor fireplace is lit each evening. Wood, leather, and marble details adjacent to large windows create a feeling of space and light. As a finishing touch, tasteful art and art books are placed near the glowing hearth.

Address AC Hotel, 260 West 40th Street, 21st Floor, New York, NY 10018, +1 (929)396-3135, www.castellnyc.com, info@castellnyc.com | Getting there Subway to Times Square–42nd Street (Line 1, 2, 3, N, Q, R, W), to 42nd Street–Port Authority Bus Terminal (Line A, C, E), or bus M 20 to 8th Avenue/West 39th Street | Hours Sun–Thu 4–11pm, Fri & Sat 4pm–midnight | Tip Take the time to listen carefully for sound artist Max Neuhaus' 1977 subtle installation called "Times Square." He created a machine that amplifies the noise from inside a subway tunnel and projects it up through the metal grate at the north end of the triangular pedestrian island on Broadway between 45th and 46th Streets (www.diaart.org/visit/visit/max-neuhaus-times-square).

32 CATCH Roof

Top-shelf seafood on an elegant outdoor terrace

In 1898, refrigeration was cutting-edge technology. Suddenly, meat, fruit, eggs, dairy, and even furs could be stored. Seizing the opportunity, the Manhattan Refrigerating Company (MRC) built a 1.6-million-square-foot business in nine adjoining buildings to service the flourishing Meatpacking District, Gansevoort Market, and Washington Market. MRC operated until 1979, a year before the last train stopped running on the neighboring High Line. Most of the meatpacking businesses have since left the area, ironically replaced by luxury brand stores.

The Meatpacking District is still dotted with landmarked buildings and Belgian block cobbled streets. It is a magnet for the late-night club scene, and is also a fantastic daytime destination. Enjoy the world-class collection at the Whitney Museum of American Art. Shop for high-end fashion and accessories in Jeffrey New York's swank mini department store. Watch the sunset from the High Line elevated park. But when your stomach is rumbling and your tired feet scream for a break, CATCH Roof is the destination for a modern, relaxed, and well-prepared rooftop meal.

CATCH Roof, situated on the fourth floor of an historic building, has a stylish outdoor terrace where guests sit under enormous shade umbrellas on smart striped green-and-white cushions next to delicate Japanese maples and climbing grape vines. A full restaurant menu features seafood, and mixologists create an array of tempting drink options at the full bar.

Open weekdays for lunch, daily for dinner, and Saturdays and Sundays for brunch, CATCH Roof also keeps the party going all night long. Late on Wednesday through Saturday nights, the curtain around the DJ booth is drawn back, and the indoor speakers and lights transform CATCH Roof into a happening lounge until 4am, while the outdoor terrace serves as a place to cool off and CATCH up with friends.

Address 21 Ninth Avenue, 4th Floor, New York, NY 10014, +1 (212)392-5978, www.catchrestaurants.com/catchroof, canycinfo@catchhg.com | Getting there Subway to 14th Street (Line A, C, E), or bus M11, M12 to Hudson Street/West 13th Street | Hours See website for hours including brunch and nightlife service | Tip Go where the locals go for daytime coffee and nighttime cocktails at Kobrick Coffee Co. (24 Ninth Avenue, New York, NY 10014, +1 (212)255-5588, www.kobricks.com).

33__City Ice Pavilion
Glide on a sky-high ice rink!

Let's say you happen to have an ice-hockey-loving child with no convenient practice rink. You also just happen to also own a warehouse with an enormous, empty rooftop. That's how City Ice Pavilion came to exist and why it is, to this day, such a hockey-centric – and an NHL-regulation size – rink. In the industrial section of Long Island City, under the 40-foot-tall, 40,000-pound air dome is New York City's only rooftop skating destination.

Twenty-four hours a day, air is blown into the fabric dome to keep it from collapsing, while three shifts of engineers make sure the complex behind-the-scenes refrigeration equipment keeps the ice from melting. They also operate one of the two Zamboni ice resurfacer machines. To support the weight of the mechanical equipment and the ice surface, and to keep the air-filled dome anchored securely so it doesn't fly away, this roof had to be reinforced with steel beams.

Hockey teams from near and far compete at City Ice Pavilion, just a stone's throw from the 59th Street Bridge that connects Long Island City with Manhattan. But if you're a casual skater, you too can experience this rooftop rink. Limited public skating sessions happen on Wednesdays and Sundays, with adults-only Coffee Club sessions happening weekday mornings for an hour and twenty minutes. Coffee is included in the price of admission.

It's easy to access via public transport, and for drivers, there is even free parking on a first-come-first-served basis. Skaters enter at street level and take the elevator to the second floor to pay admission, find bathrooms, and then visit the coffee and hot chocolate vending machine. On the third floor are two rinks: the 200' × 85' regulation size ice and the studio rink, a much smaller practice area where you can work on your triple Lutz even when the large rink is unavailable. Bring your own skates or rent a pair.

Address 47-32 32nd Place, Long Island City, NY 11101, +1 (718)706-6667, www.cityicepavilion.com | **Getting there** Subway to 33rd Street (Line 7) | **Hours** Public skate: Wed noon–1:50pm & 2–3:50pm, Sun 11:40am–1:10pm & 1:20–2:20pm; Coffee Club: Mon–Fri 8:30–9:50am | **Tip** Goodwill Industries around the corner (47–47 Van Dam Street, Long Island City, NY 11101, www.goodwill.org) sells donated clothing, shoes, and handbags by the pound. Every two hours fresh bins are brought out, and the competition is fierce.

34_City Vineyard

A glass of wine at sunset on the city's edge

Spend the day enjoying all sorts of outdoor activities in Hudson River Park. Jogging, walking, biking, miniature golfing, skateboarding, taking your puppy to the dog run, or watching your kids romp in a fantasy playground will keep you moving all day. Dancing to live music on Christopher Street Pier or socializing on an historic boat might fill your evening. But here's a combination that can't be beat: kayaking free-of-charge on the Hudson at the Downtown Boathouse located on Pier 26, and then heading upstairs to the rooftop at City Vineyard for a glass of wine, a cold beer, or a cocktail and a light bite at sunset.

During the summer months, City Vineyard is open weekdays in the late afternoons, and earlier for brunch on weekends. Although a fairly large rooftop, this popular destination has definitely been discovered. To get a seat, plan ahead and get there early, as no reservations are taken for the rooftop. City Vineyard is across the street from Citigroup's headquarters, so after business hours the bankers keep this rooftop hopping, and on the weekend, neighborhood locals cannot resist the casual atmosphere, good food, delicious drinks, and the gorgeous view.

You'll find a greeter at the bottom of the stairs who will make sure that your entire party is present before sending you up to get a table. Or perhaps a seat at the look-through bar interests you as it offers views past the bartending area directly across the Hudson River. Another plus of sitting at the bar is that you'll probably get your drink served faster when you're closer to the bartender during the busier times. And of course, while waiting on your barstool, you can count the boats on the Hudson as they sail past.

Come to City Vineyard for the American fare, the reasonably priced drinks, or the sociable atmosphere but stay for the daytime, nighttime, and especially the sunset views.

Address Pier 26 at Hudson River Park, 233 West Street, New York, NY 10013, +1 (646)677-8350, www.cityvineyardnyc.com, info@cityvineyardnyc.com | Getting there Subway to Franklin Street (Line 1), to Canal Street (Line A, C, E), to Chambers Street (Line 1, 2, 3), bus M20, M22 to Hudson Street/North Moore Street, or bus X7, X9 to West Street/North Moore Street | Hours Mon–Fri 4pm–close, Sat & Sun 1pm–close during summer months in good weather | Tip Just south at Pier 25 find beach volleyball courts, mini golf, a skate park, and Grand Banks, situated on the *Sherman Zwicker*, the largest wooden sailing ship docked in Manhattan, where you can climb onboard for drinks and light fare (cross at North Moore Street, www.hudsonriverpark.org/explore-the-park/locations/pier-25).

35__ The Crown

Above the fray at Chinatown's only rooftop bar

It took until the summer of 2017 for Chinatown to get its first roof-top bar, and it was worth the wait for the spectacular views on display. The Crown, 21 floors up in the low-rise neighborhood, rests atop the Hotel 50 Bowery. Paying homage to the local culture, the cocktails feature Chinatown ingredients: dragon fruit, papaya, lychee, and tam-arind. Two comfortable outdoor terraces that are open all summer are bridged by an indoor year-round lounge decorated with a distinct nod to mid-century modern tastes.

The larger, South-facing, triangular, outdoor space is a true bridge lover's dream come true. Simply look down to take in the Beaux Arts-inspired approach to the Manhattan Bridge for a perspec-tive that is rarely seen. Then in the distance, spy the stately Brook-lyn Bridge, the bike-friendly Williamsburg Bridge, the Triborough Bridge connecting Queens and the Bronx, and the Queensboro/59th Street Bridge. The smaller, North-facing terrace overlooks the city toward the Empire State and Chrysler buildings and may be the best spot for enjoying the sunset. From this unique Chinatown aerie, you can see Manhattan, Brooklyn, and the silhouettes of Queens, the Bronx, and New Jersey in the distance.

Both terraces have low cushioned sofas for small groups. If you'd like to be assured of an outdoor seat, remember to make a reservation. The glass parapet keeps guests safe while maintaining the wide-open vista. On both terraces, it is much quieter than inside the connecting indoor lounge that has DJs spinning tunes and keeping the party go-ing on weekend nights.

Down on the second floor of the hotel is a sprawling outdoor ter-race called Atlantic Garden. When not booked for a private soirée, this elevated space is worth a look on your way up to the rooftop bar. However, The Crown's outdoor terraces truly are the jewels in Hotel 50 Bowery's sparkling tiara.

Address Hotel 50 Bowery, 50 Bowery, 21st Floor, New York, NY 10013, +1 (646)630-8057, www.thecrownnyc.com, gia@3krg.com | Getting there Subway to Canal Street (Line 4, 5, 6, J, N, Q, R, W, Z), to Grand Street (Line B, D), or bus M 103 to Bowery/Canal Street | Hours Mon–Wed 10am–midnight, Thu & Fri 10–2am, Sat noon–2am, Sun noon–midnight | Tip Delight in the unusual at The Original Chinatown Ice Cream Factory with "regular" flavors such as lychee, durian, red bean, and taro, while the "exotic" flavors list includes strawberry, chocolate, and vanilla (65 Bayard Street, New York, NY 10013, www.chinatownicecreamfactory.com).

36__DaDong

DaDong goes west to DaApple

When First Lady Michelle Obama visited Beijing, she dined at DaDong. It's known for Peking duck, a Chinese delicacy invented more than seven centuries ago during the Yuan Dynasty. The bird is roasted until the skin is lacquered and crispy, and the meat is succulent and sweet, artfully carved off the bone. Traditionally, the duck is dressed with scallions and hoisin sauce, then wrapped in a thin pancake, creating a luscious dish.

One of the popular purveyors of Peking duck in China is DaDong, a chain of restaurants named after its imposing chef's pet moniker. Dong Zhenxiang, owner of DaDong, is, by all accounts, a tall man. In Chinese, *da* is the word for "big," and because of his imposing stature, China's lauded chef is fondly referred to as "DaDong." In 2018, DaDong restaurants expanded out of the East, and headed west, amid great fanfare, to "DaApple," New York City.

Chef Dong practices *YiJing* Cuisine, where food is edible art. Each beautiful dish interprets an associated Chinese poem. In the New York location, all three levels of the 17,500-square-foot restaurant exhibit modern Chinese painting and sculpture for a fully immersive experience.

On the second floor, the stylish and comfortable terrace garden seats more than 150 guests. Outdoors is a full bar, a raw seafood bar, attentive service, and a central reflecting pool framing a striking stainless-steel sculpture of water in motion. Get closer to notice that it's made out of stylized Chinese characters, which undoubtedly are words of a poem.

Wednesday and Thursday from 5 to 8pm, enjoy another art form, live jazz, while savoring Asian-inspired bar bites and perhaps a smoking Enter the Dragon cocktail, or any dish from the full menu at the outdoor garden terrace tables or lounge seats. Lunch, dinner, and weekend brunch can be served outside, and DaDong's outdoor heaters extend the elevated terrace's season.

Address 3 Bryant Park, New York, NY 10036, +1 (212)355-9600, www.dadongny.com, info@dadongny.com | Getting there Subway to 42nd Street–Bryant Park (Line 7, B, D, F, M), or bus M 5, M 7, M 42, M 55 to West 42nd Street/Sixth Avenue | Hours Mon–Sat 11:30am–11pm, Sun 11:30am–10:30pm | Tip Across the street is the Stephen A. Schwarzman Building, the lauded Main Branch of the New York Public Library, with its entrance flanked by the Library Lions, named Patience and Fortitude. Take a free one-hour tour that includes the Rose Main Reading Room (476 Fifth Avenue, New York, NY 10018, www.nypl.org).

37__ The Eagle NYC

The West Side's gay story

In 2001, when The Eagle NYC reopened on West 28th Street between 10th and 11th Avenues, it was a remote, even dangerous location, and perfect for a gay leather bar. Today, that same block is unrecognizable. With the Zaha Hadid-designed apartment building at one end of the street and the Rolls-Royce dealership at the other, plus art galleries and more luxury housing in-between, just about the only remnant of the pre-High Line West Side is The Eagle NYC.

From sailors to Stonewall, the history of the Eagle Bar reveals the evolving story of Manhattan's West Side. Back in 1931, the original Eagle Open Kitchen served as a longshoremen's pub on 11th Avenue. After the 1969 Stonewall riots in Greenwich Village opened the door for gay bars, The Eagle's Nest was officially reincarnated as a gay men's leather bar, with black walls and a grungy motorcycle parked inside. This burly men's bar wasn't just for cruising. It sponsored community-based gay sports teams, raised money for a local AIDS clinic at its weekly Tea Dances, and created a float for the annual Gay Pride Parade. In 1980, the bar was featured in an Al Pacino film, *Cruising*. However, by 2000, the area was gentrifying, and rents were going up. And so, after 49 years, The Eagle closed its history-laden doors.

In 2001, the phoenix rose from the ashes when a new owner opened another Eagle in what was a 19th-century stable, just a few blocks from the original bar. He imported the black-walled, dimly lit décor and the thumping music, and even displayed the dilapidated motorcycle from the original Eagle in this much larger space.

In good weather, the 2,000-square-foot roof deck is the place to enjoy a drink, a smoke, or do what Pacino did in the movie – cruise for burly he-men. The formerly private roof deck is now on view to those in the luxury high-rise apartment building across the street.

Address 554 West 28th Street, New York, NY 10001, +1 (646)473-1866, www.eagle-ny.com, info@eagle-ny.com | Getting there Subway to 34th Street–Hudson Yards (Line 7), or bus M12 to 11th Avenue/West 29th Street | Hours Mon–Wed 10pm–4am, Thu–Sat 7pm–4am, Sun 5pm–4am | Tip Porchlight is a lively, street-level bar that serves Southern-inspired cocktails paired with comfort food. Enjoy a Damn Fine Rusty Nail and some warm bourbon bar nuts (271 Eleventh Avenue, New York, NY 10001, www.porchlightbar.com).

38 Eataly Birreria

The name, décor, and menu changes with the seasons

Birreria, the rooftop restaurant above Eataly, has different names for its summer and winter offerings. Wearing a woolen scarf and boots? Then it's BAITA, a tasty slice of the Italian Alps at the rooftop bar, restaurant and microbrewery above Eataly, the all-things-Italian destination market in the Flatiron District. The retractable roof will be shuttered for the winter, and the ski lodge décor will reflect the northern Italian food and bar menu.

But when shorts and sandals are the style of the day, the retractable roof at SERRA is opened, revealing a bird's-eye view of the famous clock tower and gold finial atop the Met Life Tower. Italian for "greenhouse," SERRA's retractable open roof lets in natural light that streams past dozens of artificial but realistic-looking hanging plants. And the farm-to-table menu reflects exactly what's in season in the Union Square Greenmarket several blocks down Broadway because that is where the vast majority of the produce on the menu comes from.

Executive Chef Jackie Jeong totes her enormous handcart to the farmer's market each Monday, Wednesday, Friday, and Saturday at 8am, the hour when scores of local chefs shop. When it's tomato or squash season, she says she often carts back as much as 1,000 pounds of fresh produce – all on her own! The list of farmers and producers she frequents is painted on the wall for all to see.

BAITA or SERRA, year-round Birreria, Italian for "brewery," is busy making beer. The only rooftop microbrewery in New York City and for which this rooftop restaurant is named is tucked away in the corner, but the homemade brews are served on tap at the long bar. You can also enjoy seasonal cocktails made with natural infusions, or the lemonade bar where guests choose from three varieties of lemon, an array of herbal infused simple syrups, and for over-21s, herb-infused spirits. *Cin cin!*

Address Eataly, 200 Fifth Avenue, 13th Floor, New York, NY 10010, +1 (212)937-8910, www.eataly.com/us_en/stores/nyc-flatiron/serra-by-birreria | Getting there Subway to 23rd Street (Line N, Q, R, W), or bus M1, M2, M3, M55 to Fifth Avenue/23rd Street | Hours Daily 11:30am–11pm | Tip On the last Friday of each month, Birreria hosts a midnight rooftop speakeasy which requires a secret password to enter. Up to two weeks in advance, you can send an email requesting the password and a reservation (socialmedia@eataly.com).

39 __ Elevated Acre

Evoking the beauty of the Hamptons in Manhattan

Bring your earbuds to this somewhat hard-on-the-ears but easy-on-the-eyes elevated garden. Located more than 30 feet above South Street and the noisy FDR lies a wood-planked, beach-style boardwalk and nearby dunes bursting with flora native to the Hamptons. Though the Elevated Acre is not in plain sight, intrepid explorers are handsomely rewarded when they discover this exceptional space.

One of just three above-ground "Publicly Owned Private Spaces" (POPS) in Manhattan, the Elevated Acre was given new life when it reopened in 2005 after a three-year, $7-million renovation.

If some of the Acre's elements, including the exceptional lighting, the use of native plant species, and the modern seating, feel vaguely familiar, give yourself a gold star for noticing. Landscape architect Ken Smith designed this project just a few years before he collaborated on the nearby green-roofed Pier 15 and the East River Esplanade.

Although the Elevated Acre is sandwiched in by the 13-story 55 Water Street office building and the 54-story south tower, expansive vistas of the Brooklyn Bridge, the East River, Governors Island, and Pier 6's heliport are there for the taking at this above-ground garden and performance art venue.

In the middle of the Elevated Acre is an artificial turf-lined amphitheater that is one of the homes of the annual River to River Festival. Free films and dozens of other cultural events happen here each summer.

While a beautiful spot for the garden and views by day, the Elevated Acre has a different feel when the sun goes down. At dusk, the focal point becomes the 50-foot, glowing lantern constructed of translucent glass that is built on the northeast corner. A certain mood creator for people on the Elevated Acre, the changing colored lights also act as a beacon for boats floating up the East River, as well as for people walking along the Brooklyn Promenade.

Address 55 Water Street, New York, NY 10041, www.55water.com/building/amenities/
elevated-acre | **Getting there** Subway to Wall Street (Line 2, 3), to Whitehall Street South
Ferry (Line R), to Broad Street (Line J, Z), to Bowling Green (Line 4, 5), or bus M 15
to Water Street/Hanover Square | **Hours** Daily 8am–9pm | **Tip** In 1658, the first street
in Manhattan was paved with stones. Today Stone Street is a great food and drink
destination, especially in the summer when the spirited pedestrian-only throughway is filled
with shaded outdoor tables (Stone Street, New York, NY 10004, www.cityroverwalks.com/
stone-street-nyc).

40__Elsewhere

Where underground music and art goes upstairs

A lot of cool stuff happens on three levels, including The Rooftop, at Elsewhere, home to a diverse Brooklyn crowd that appreciates emerging bands, DJs, and multimedia artists. Elsewhere's stated mission is, "Creative risk-taking, progressive music programming, respect for all people and art, and a desire to support and grow the communities that make it all possible."

Actualizing that mission happens in a repurposed Bushwick warehouse located in an industrial neighborhood where space is abundant. Late-night noise restrictions are not a factor, so the party, even on the outdoor rooftop, can continue without annoying the sleep-seeking neighbors.

Insiders know to check the events calendar before going, as there is always something new happening. RSVP if necessary, arrive early, and leave plenty of time to explore, as Elsewhere often has simultaneous events. The Hall and Zone One are indoor spaces for music, parties and immersive art installations. The Loft is a hangout for coffee, free Wi-Fi, snacks, and happy hour Tuesdays to Fridays. Rotating art installations happen in The Courtyard and on The Skybridge.

The latest addition to Elsewhere is The Rooftop, a warm-weather venue with a distant view of the Manhattan skyline. It easily accommodates 500 people with its state-of-the-art sound system and outdoor bar offering the requisite rooftop frozen drink options and light fare.

On Tuesdays, The Rooftop is dedicated to experimental events, film, food, and art. Wednesdays and Thursdays have no-cover DJ parties. Fridays, Saturdays, and Sundays host ticketed shows and parties. RSVP in advance, and rooftop admission is free between 2 and 4pm each Friday, Saturday, and Sunday. Picnic tables or bar-side stools and the aerial sailcloth triangles that create some shade make this open-air rooftop a great place to hang out. When the crowds arrive, the party begins.

Address 599 Johnson Avenue, Brooklyn, NY 11237, www.elsewherebrooklyn.com, info@elsewherebrooklyn.com | **Getting there** Subway to Jefferson Street (Line L), or bus B 57 to Flushing Avenue / Cypress Avenue | **Hours** The Rooftop is open seasonally Tue–Wed 5pm–1am, Thu–Sat 5pm–2am, Sun 2pm–1am | **Tip** Express your creativity at House of Yes where circus, dance, theater, and cabaret performances invite all to live out their party fantasies (2 Wyckoff Avenue, Brooklyn, NY 11237, www.houseofyes.org).

41 __ Elsie Rooftop

A suitably lavish place for Jazz Age drinks

Back in the day, an invitation to one of Elsie de Wolfe's fabulous soirées, whether in London, New York, or Paris, was quite the social coup. A woman of immense style and charm, Elsie de Wolfe (1865–1950) was a closely watched trendsetter who is credited with becoming the first professional interior designer. In 1913, her best-selling book on home design, *A House in Good Taste*, was published. The text and photos, compiled from articles Ms. de Wolfe had penned for magazines of her day, offered advice so timeless the book was reprinted 90 years later in 2004.

This Jazz Age rooftop bar pays homage to Elsie's legacy of "Suitability, Simplicity and Proportion," the title of the second chapter in her book. Though in the middle of manic Midtown Manhattan, it is hidden away on the twenty-fifth floor of a nondescript office building, and just high enough to feel like an elegant world far from the Fashion District fray below.

To evoke its stylish namesake, the interior, done in lush pastels accented with gold, is *trés elegant*. A spacious, comfortable, and charming wraparound flower garden terrace completes the bar. The office building penthouse that has been so lavishly transformed into Elsie Rooftop is a sophisticated, year-round, after-work, pre- or post-theater, or Saturday brunch destination.

As one would expect from an exceptional hostess, Elsie Rooftop offers signature bespoke cocktails, including the namesake Elsie de Wolfe, made from vodka, cucumber, lemon, and sparkling rosé, as well as a hand-selected wine menu. Exceptional small plates have been designed by chef David Burke, almost as carefully as if Elsie herself had planned the menu.

For a rooftop bar that offers an all-season elevated experience, gents, spend a moment to straighten your ties, and, ladies, check that the seams in your stockings are straight before entering.

Address 1412 Broadway, 25th Floor, New York, NY 10018, +1 (212)764-1090, www.elsierooftop.com, info@elsierooftop.com | **Getting there** Subway to Times Square–42nd Street (Line 1, 2, 3, N, Q, R, W), to 42nd Street–Port Authority Bus Terminal (Line A, C, E), to Grand Central–42nd Street (Line 4, 5, 6, 7, S), or bus M5, M7, M55 to Avenue of the Americas (Sixth Avenue)/West 40th Street | **Hours** Mon–Sat 4pm–close, check website for Sat brunch hours | **Tip** Sip hot chocolate and watch ice skaters glide to nostalgic American songbook tunes at Bryant Park's Winter Village from Halloween through the beginning of March (daily 8am – 10pm; Bryant Park, between 40th and 42nd Streets & Fifth and Sixth Avenues, New York, NY 10018, www.bryantpark.org).

42_ The Empire Rooftop

Start any day with a rooftop breakfast

The Empire Rooftop, an expansive indoor-outdoor rooftop lounge, serves up delicious cocktails every day of the year, has a weekend DJ spinning tunes, and always has terrific views – but so do several other New York City roof bars. Well, one of its truly unique aspects is that The Empire Rooftop serves breakfast and weekend brunch. Fresh squeezed orange juice, French toast with maple syrup and thick cut bacon on a New York City rooftop overlooking the Metropolitan Opera House in Lincoln Center is one of the best ways to start any day anywhere.

If breakfast leaves you wanting more time up here, swing by during happy hour from 4 to 7pm each Monday through Friday for a bite and a reasonably priced libation at the only rooftop bar on the Upper West Side. The tasteful decorations, friendly wait staff, and terrific neighborhood views invite you to unwind at the end of your work or stay-cation day. Later in the evening, the velvet rope goes up, and it gets a little louder and dressier as the bar turns into a popular party destination. After 8pm, it's prudent to make a reservation, especially on Friday and Saturday nights when the DJ plays.

Under the retro glow of the red neon Empire Hotel signs on the west-facing terrace, enjoy views over Central Park and Lincoln Center for a song. But there's more! Depending on how much you are willing to spend, The Empire has two additional roof elevations. Between Memorial Day and Labor Day, up the ante, book a room, and gain access to the 150-person capacity Pool Deck with its plunge pool and sun beds. When you want the deluxe rooftop experience, reserve a private cabana with an iPod docking station, plasma screen TV, a personal refrigerator, and free wireless internet on the roof level a few steps below the pool. For those who feel the need to unwind even further, arrange for an outdoor rooftop massage through the hotel's spa.

Address The Empire Hotel, 44 West 63rd Street, 12th Floor, New York, NY 10023, +1 (212)265-2600, www.empirehotelnyc.com | **Getting there** Subway to 59th Street–Columbus Circle (Line 1, A, B, C, D), or 66th Street–Lincoln Center (Line 1) | **Hours** Breakfast: daily 7–10:30am; brunch: Sat & Sun 11am–3pm; bar: Mon–Wed 3pm–1am, Thu & Fri 3pm–2am, Sat 11–2am, Sun 11–1am | **Tip** The David Rubenstein Atrium (61 West 62nd Street, New York, NY 10023, www.atrium.lincolncenter.org) is open daily and offers a lovely indoor place to get out of the cold or heat. See free performances every Thursday at 7:30pm.

43__Empire State Building

New York City's most beloved outdoor roof terrace

Nothing symbolizes New York City better than the Empire State Building. Other rooftops featured throughout this book frequently boast views of this art deco masterpiece. It may no longer be the tallest building in the world, or even in New York City, but it remains the most iconic one. Its famous rooftop is frequented by millions of visitors.

Every night the tower lights come on. A computer-driven LED light system was installed in 2012. With16 million colors, the lighting displays have become much more elaborate. The tower can also sport special effects, like a bright red heartbeat on Valentine's Day or multi-colored, twinkling lights on New Year's Eve.

Since its completion in 1931, the Empire State Building has been in scores of movies, making it the most recognizable skyscraper ever built. Oddly enough, the most famous movie star to visit the building never actually set foot, or paw, on the site. In the 1933 movie, *King Kong*, a fictional giant ape climbed the exterior of what was then the world's tallest skyscraper – but only with the help of movie-making magicians in Hollywood, thousands of miles from New York City.

Join the more than 120 million visitors who have taken the ear popping, high-speed elevators to 86th floor Observatory. This skyward trip is thrilling but secure, fast, and easy, especially when tickets are purchased in advance.

There is an alternate way to reach the Observatory: take the stairs! Each year since 1978, hundreds of hopeful athletes enter a lottery to win a chance to race up the 86 flights and 1,576 steps. The women's record is 11:23, and the men's is 9:33. This annual charity Run-Up event is organized by NYCRUNS.

Whether you ride the elevators today or plan to sprint up the steps next year, make sure to experience New York City's most beloved roof terrace. On a clear day, the views are spectacular and almost infinite.

Address 350 Fifth Avenue, New York, NY 10118, +1 (212)736-3100, www.esbnyc.com |
Getting there Subway to 34th Street–Herald Square (Line B, D, F, M, N, Q, R, W), or
bus M 1, M 2, M 3, M 5, M 55, BxM 3, BxM 4 to Fifth Avenue/West 33rd Street | **Hours**
Daily 8–2am | **Tip** Just a short walk downtown is a "tree museum" in Madison Square
Park. Located just across from the iconic Flatiron Building, this park is an accredited
arboretum with over 300 trees, as well as an impressive public art program (between
Broadway, Madison Avenue, East 23rd Street and East 26th Street, New York, NY 10010,
www.madisonsquarepark.org/mad-sq-hort/trees).

44 Empire Stores

One roof, two bejeweled bridges

The Brooklyn Bridge and the Manhattan Bridge, the elegant and beloved spans connecting the boroughs, get dolled up every night. When the sun goes down, strings of bulbs light up, and from a distance, it appears that both bridges are wearing shimmering pearl necklaces.

The rooftop at Empire Stores, open nightly until 1am, offers this exact view from between the bridges, across the East River and into the million dots of light that make up the Manhattan skyline.

Day or night, the Empire Stores roof is a peaceful, easily accessible destination where fresh air, inspiring views, and comfortable day-bed-style seating abound. Choose from the stairs or the stylish glass elevator to reach the fifth floor where beautiful plantings adorn the 21st-century rooftop built inside the walls of this Civil War-era coffee warehouse.

This warehouse is only one of what was once a nearly three-mile stretch of similar structures along the Brooklyn waterfront that serviced the world's then-busiest shipping ports. It is one of the few remaining warehouses left with period details such as star-shaped cast-iron anchor plates attached to tie-rod braces used back then in brick buildings to prevent the walls from spreading apart. Dozens of symmetrical arched windows with beautiful brickwork and metal shutters, schist stone walls, and heavy frame timber construction give timeless charm to the façade of Empire Stores.

Achieving LEED Silver status, the hip interior has been constructed in an environmentally conscious style. Amenities, such as cafés, high-end retail, and premium office space are topped off by the fifth-floor 7,000-square-foot public garden. Most often, the roof is a destination to relax and enjoy the view, but from time to time, sunrise and sunset yoga, boot camp fitness, and even cycling classes happen in this 19th-century-meets-21st-century open-air oasis.

Address 55 Water Street, Brooklyn, NY 11201, www.empirestoresdumbo.com | Getting there Subway to York Street (Line F), to High Street (Line A, C), to Clark Street (Line 2, 3), or bus B25 to Water Street/Main Street | Hours Daily 6–1am | Tip Brooklyn Historical Society DUMBO, located inside the Empire Stores building, has a great deal more information on local history, including this Civil War-era coffee warehouse (55 Water Street, Brooklyn, NY 11201, +1 (718)222-4111, www.brooklynhistory.org).

45 __Fort Tompkins & Battery Weed

The oldest green roofs in New York City

Fort Wadsworth, strategically located on the southeastern shore of Staten Island, has guarded the entrance of the New York Harbor since George Washington was president over 200 years ago. It is the fort with the longest continuous military use in the United States and is listed on the National Register of Historic Places. It is also where 50,000 runners gather for the start of the annual New York City Marathon each November. The fort's grounds surround the approach to the Verrazano-Narrows Bridge, which connects Staten Island to Brooklyn, and the views from Fort Wadsworth itself are awe-inspiring.

Within the fort are two green-roofed structures dating back to the mid-1800s. Directly on the harbor is Battery Weed, a catacomb-like, three-tiered granite structure capable of firing more than 116 cannons at once. This trapezoidal fortification lies on the water's edge where the Atlantic meets New York's harbor.

On the bluff above, protecting Battery Weed, is the other green-roofed structure called Fort Tompkins. Serving as a barracks and a fortification, it has a fascinating design-built rooftop water collection system to ensure soldiers inside had access to clean water, even if they became trapped inside for an extended period. Fortunately, this fort never took enemy fire, so the process was never truly tested. Today, Battery Weed and Fort Tompkins are home to myriad thriving plants and shrubs.

The Fort Tompkins building is not generally open to visitors, but if you catch one of the Park Rangers on a quiet day and express genuine interest in the Fort Tompkins rooftop, he or she may take you on a guided tour of the water cisterns inside the structure and perhaps even up to the roof to see where the centuries-old water collection system begins.

Address Fort Wadsworth, 210 New York Avenue, Staten Island, NY 10305,
+1 (718)354-4500, www.nyharborparks.org | **Getting there** From St. George Ferry take
bus S 51 or S 81 to Bay Street/Lyman Avenue | **Hours** Wed–Sun 10am–4:30pm | **Tip**
On certain full-moonlit nights and for a small fee, you can further explore the 226-acre fort
by taking the two-hour ranger-led Lantern Tour. Plus, if you just can't face rushing back to
the urban hustle and bustle, Fort Wadsworth offers overnight camping.

46__Gallow Green
Creating the romance of Scotland – plus cocktails

In 1939, weeks before opening the grandest hotel Manhattan had ever seen, World War II erupted, and The McKittrick Hotel was shuttered until 2011. That's just one of the fabulously inventive stories upon which the immersive theater experience, "Sleep No More," is based.

The show's wordless storyline is about Shakespeare's most superstitious tragedy, *Macbeth*, known as "the Scottish play" by those unwilling to even utter the doomed king's name. Warehouse turned theater, McKittrick is another nod to a Scottish family name dating back to 1376, as well as a wink to Hitchcock's film noir, *Vertigo*. The rooftop bar, Gallow Green, invokes a tale of a storied village a few miles south of Glasgow which gained notoriety from the stabbing and burning of the "Paisley Witches" in 1697.

So it's no surprise that, when entering the McKittrick Hotel and taking the creaky elevator to the top floor, it magically whisks you to a weathered country rail station, so overgrown that it has almost gone to seed in the most charming way possible. It is helplessly romantic, whimsical, and rustically elegant.

Sleep No More-inspired cocktails and their magical signature punches served in large copper bowls are offered all summer. The twinkling lights and varied seating areas, with a swing for intimate pairings and an abandoned rail car for large groups, continue the vintage ambience that jettisons guests to another era. The open-air, overgrown rooftop garden is perfect for dinner, drinks, jazz brunch, sunset Sunday world music, and even a monthly Saturday morning children's tea, teddy bears included!

Each winter, the roof is changed into a Scottish *bothe*. In this mountainside lodge, cozy up next to the fire pit, stretch out on bunk beds, or venture outside to the rooftop pine forest as you are transported from New York City to the wilderness of the Scottish Highlands.

Address McKittrick Hotel, 542 West 27th Street, NY 10001, +1 (212)564-1662, www.mckittrickhotel.com/gallow-green, gallowgreen@mckittrickhotel.com | Getting there Subway to 23rd Street (Line C, E), to 28th Street (Line 1), bus M 12 to 11th Avenue/ West 26th Street, or bus M 11 to 10th Avenue/West 27th Street | Hours Daily 5pm–close, Sat brunch 11am–4pm | Tip Chelsea has a plethora of art galleries between 10th and 11th Avenues from West 21st Street to West 27th street that are free to explore; just remember that most are closed on Sundays (www.chelseagallerymap.com).

47 __ Garden of Stones
Rooftop Holocaust Memorial

Anything is possible on a New York City rooftop, including a fantastic art installation. The Museum of Jewish Heritage in Battery Park City hosts this exceptional, 4,150-square-foot rooftop garden, overflowing with symbolism and beauty. It was created by the celebrated British artist Andy Goldsworthy.

Goldsworthy is known for using natural materials, and Garden of Stones is no exception. Commissioned by the Museum of Jewish Heritage as a "contemplative space dedicated to the memory of those who perished in the Holocaust and a tribute to those who survived," it is no accident that this rooftop memorial has an uninterrupted view across the water to the Statue of Liberty.

In 2003, each of the 18 specially chosen, prepared, and hollowed boulders was planted with a single dwarf oak sapling. Over time, the trees will continue to grow inside the three-to-thirteen-ton boulders, roots fusing to the stone, fusing the strongest of natural elements to the most fragile. While beautiful in all seasons, perhaps the most spectacular time to view this installation is after a light dusting of snow when the drama of the boulders and the young singleton trees struggling through the winter against a background of gray skies is at its height.

Goldsworthy's works, including this remarkably moving design, his only permanent New York City installation, explore the effect of time on humans and nature. In order to document change in the Garden of Stones, a time-lapse camera is installed above the garden. "Timekeeper" compiles these photos and allows museum visitors to see the garden from its inception, being planted with tiny saplings, through the leafy and bare seasons, through snow and heat, and over years until today. After your visit in the garden, head inside where you can easily find yourself memorialized in this time-lapsed record.

Address Museum of Jewish Heritage, 36 Battery Place, New York, NY 10280, +1 (646)437-4202, www.mjhnyc.org | Getting there Subway to Bowling Green (Line 4, 5), to Rector Street (Line 1, R), to South Ferry (Line 1), or to Whitehall Street – South Ferry (Line R, W) | Hours Sun – Tue 10am – 5:45pm, Wed & Thu 10am – 8pm, Fri 10am – 5pm (see website for winter hours on Fridays Nov–Mar), eve of major Jewish holidays 10am – 3pm | Tip The shady, 2-acre Teardrop Park is an oasis of natural discovery with a rock grotto, a slide, and a fountain in which kids can play (Warren Street between River Terrace and North End Avenue, New York, NY 10005, www.bpcparks.org).

48_ Good Behavior

Good times where bad things used to happen

In 1876, so the story goes, New York cop Captain "Clubber" Williams took so many bribes from the brothels, gambling houses, saloons, dance halls, and "clip joints" in his new precinct that he is famous for saying, "I've been having chuck steak ever since I've been on the force, and now I'm going to have a bit of tenderloin." Thus, the name Tenderloin was given to the late 19th-century vice district of Manhattan. It stretched between 24th Street and 42nd Street and from Fifth Avenue to Seventh Avenue. Early 20th-century reformers labeled this section of Manhattan known for bad behavior as "Satan's Circus."

Well over a century later, "Clubber" Williams and the vice he profited so handsomely from are long gone. The neighborhood has a shiny new name: NoMad, short for North of Madison Square Park. This is where you'll find the inviting 18th-floor roof bar, Good Behavior at MADE Hotel, built where so much bad behavior once occurred. The rooftop bar's Tiki-inspired cocktails are named after the graft-taking cop, famous brothels, and *The Gentleman's Directory*, a travel advisory of the day that informed men exactly where to find whatever they were looking for.

Good Behavior is a year-round, indoor-outdoor bar shaped like a water tower. The designer must have been inspired by the view from the south terrace because you can probably see more rooftop water towers from this vantage point than from any other rooftop bar in the city.

When it's warm, Good Behavior, a modern bar with lush greenery and comfortable seating, has retracting glass doors that make it a seamless, open-air venue. During winter, when the glass doors are closed, they still allow for terrific Old New York views.

Good Behavior takes no reservations and accepts no cash. They do not serve food. But the tropical drinks, inviting décor, and endless water tower views make it a must-see destination.

Address MADE Hotel, 44 West 29th Street, 18th Floor, New York, NY 10001,
+1 (212)213-4429, www.madehotels.com/eat-drink | Getting there Subway to 28th Street
(Line 1, N, R, W), or bus M7, M55 to Avenue of the Americas / West 29th Street | Hours
Sun 4pm–midnight, Mon 5–10pm, Tue–Thu 5pm–midnight, Fri 5pm–2am | Tip
Wander through New York's Flower District, a dwindling but still vibrant community of
plant wholesalers and retailers, on West 28th Street between Sixth and Seventh Avenues.
Bring cash and go early, as most stores are open Mon–Fri 5:30–10:30am.

49_ Gotham Greens
Whole Foods

Produce that couldn't be any more local if it tried

The corporate farms that grow much of our food are typically located far from cities where the vast majority of the people who eat the food actually live and shop. The result is that produce is grown and harvested in one region, then packed up and trucked to distant cities, ultimately delivering less than freshly picked produce. Your best alternative has always been shopping at your nearest greenmarket for locally grown produce.

In 2009, Brooklyn welcomed a commercial rooftop hydroponic farm. Today, high-tech, hyper-local, soil-less produce is grown on top of the grocery store where the ultra-fresh lettuce, basil, and microgreens are sold to shoppers who live within walking or biking distance. This lettuce never sees an interstate highway.

Hydroponic farming has been around for a while, but Gotham Greens' farm designer and chief agriculture officer Jennifer Nelkin Frymark earned her degree in controlled-environment agriculture. She designed the first commercially-viable system that can grow food reliably and predictably in 30- to 40-day cycles throughout our plant-killing hot New York summers and our produce-barren freezing winters. Year-round at Gotham Greens, it's delightfully warm and humid, just the way the plants like it.

But can Gotham Greens' produce grow anywhere that their proprietary greenhouse environment could be built – even in space? Yes, in fact, and NASA has been in touch with Gotham Greens.

This may be the future of food, but it is happening today in Brooklyn. Each Wednesday at 6pm you can see the rooftop farm at Whole Foods. Since it is a highly controlled environment, visitors are not permitted inside the greenhouse, but you can get a fascinating introduction to this pesticide-free, super-sustainable farming system.

Address Whole Foods, 214 Third Street, Brooklyn, NY 11215, +1 (718)935-0600, www.gothamgreens.com/our-farms/gowanus | **Getting there** Subway to Carroll Street (Line F, G), or Union Street (Line R) | **Hours** Wed 6pm; reservations are suggested but not required | **Tip** Nearby Runner & Stone is a restaurant and bar, and also a remarkable bakery. Go there to eat or pick up a loaf of their mouthwatering rye ciabatta to enjoy with your fresh salad at home (285 Third Avenue, Brooklyn, NY 11215, www.runnerandstone.com).

50__Graziella's

Italian food like Mama used to make

Sometimes what seems like bad luck is just good luck waiting to happen. Vito Randazzo, who has owned Graziella's for more than 15 years, was looking to get out of the "slice and soda" pizza business in which he grew up. First, he studied to be a pharmacist, then finance, and then he tried his hand at real estate. While looking, unsuccessfully, for a tenant for an empty garage on Vanderbilt Avenue that was owned by his girlfriend's dad, it occurred to him that the space could be turned into something the neighborhood lacked at that time: a sit-down pizza restaurant with a traditional Italian menu.

Vito gave up real estate and, with his soon-to-be father-in-law, went right back into the pizza business. This time, however, he built a family-friendly restaurant that he named after his Sicilian mother, Graziella. He added an authentic wood-burning pizza oven and has always used only fresh mozzarella, good olive oil, and natural ingredients. The restaurant even recreates some of Vito's Sicilian mama's personal recipes.

Vito's new father-in-law and new business partner is a talented carpenter who built out the restaurant, including the charming wooden roof deck. Accessed by one flight of stairs, the uncovered portion of the deck facing Vanderbilt Avenue is a cozy 12 x 24 feet with flowering planters along the perimeter. String lighting and a view of the avenue below that acts as the border between Fort Greene and Clinton Hill add to the festive atmosphere. The rear portion of the roof has a canvas ceiling and mounted fans to keep guests comfortable in warm weather.

Graziella's unpretentious deck, one of the oldest, continuously operating rooftop restaurants in New York City, is open from May through October to take advantage of outdoor weather. The rest of the year, it's worth a stop at this neighborhood classic for some excellent pizza, pasta, and good cheer.

Address 232 Vanderbilt Avenue, Brooklyn, NY 11205, +1 (718)789-5663, www.graziellasmenu.com | **Getting there** Subway to Clinton–Washington Avenues (Line G), or bus B 69 to Vanderbilt Avenue/Willoughby Avenue | **Hours** Mon–Wed 2–11pm, Thu–Sun 11am–11pm | **Tip** Find fabulous handmade clothes, house décor, and jewelry that promotes fair trade at 21Tara (388 Myrtle Avenue, Brooklyn, NY 11205, www.21tarabrooklyn.com).

51__Hauser & Wirth New York, 22nd Street

Artist-curated summer film series en plein air

International art dealers Hauser & Wirth have galleries in chic locations across the globe, including Zurich, London, Hong Kong, and two locations in New York City. One of the Manhattan spaces is in the more traditional, art-centric Upper East Side, and the other is downtown in the contemporary-focused art gallery district of Chelsea. In a spacious, repurposed, multilevel warehouse, the downtown gallery hosts exhibition space, as well as Hauser & Wirth's first dedicated book store featuring artists' books and rare volumes, plus a café located inside an art exhibit.

The Chelsea gallery is also the first Hauser & Wirth location to open its rooftop to curious art lovers, albeit on a very limited schedule, and usually requiring an advanced RSVP. Part of the gallery's mission is to engage with the community and educate art lovers of all ages. Rotating sculpture installations, the occasional immersive exhibit, and even concerts happen on their sprawling warehouse rooftop. Yet, the most popular event to date is the Artist's Choice Summer Film Series.

Each summer, in a free film series like no other, artists represented by the gallery are asked to select a single film that has inspired his or her work. Often, the selection is an underappreciated or hard-to-find cinema treasure. Communal viewing is casual as guests sit on the floor. Light fare is available. A rooftop film viewing party ensues next to the iconic cedar water tower and London-based artist Martin Creedo's eye-popping massive wall mural. Guests sit among the rooftop-installed sculptures, and all is within eyeshot of the Hudson River. Space is limited, even on a rooftop this expansive, so RSVP early, bring a blanket to sit on, and enjoy a specially chosen film amongst contemporary art in a one-of-a-kind setting.

Address 548 West 22nd Street, New York, NY 10011, +1 (212)790-3900, www.hauserwirth.com, newyork@hauserwirth.com | **Getting there** Subway to 23rd Street (Line C, E), or bus M 12 to 11th Avenue / West 23rd Street | **Hours** Gallery Tue–Sat 10am–6pm, check website for rooftop event schedule | **Tip** Eat and drink inside an art exhibit at The Roth Bar, originally constructed in 1997 entirely of salvaged materials, resurrected at Hauser & Wirth New York (548 West 22nd Street, New York, NY 10011, www.hauserwirth.com/stories/17007-roth-bar-hauser-wirth-new-york-22nd-street).

52_ The Heights

A glass terrace not for the vertigo-prone

The Heights' small but absolutely terrifying cantilevered, glass-floored terrace is not for the weak-kneed. Standing on it, you look straight down on East 31st Street with nothing to break the imaginary fall. The bar's designers took mercy on us when they left room for a simple wooden bench on either side of the see-through floor so that thrill seekers can experience this heart-in-your-throat sensation from a seated vantage point that is just a little bit less scary. Of course, a cocktail from the much safer feeling bar positioned above the hotel's secure structure helps you work up the courage to move over to the transparent floor more than 300 feet in the air.

This casual modern bar atop the Arlo NoMad Hotel belies the spectacular Manhattan experience afforded by The Heights' rooftop bar. Exiting the elevator corridor as you enter the terrace, you can't help but be dazzled by the iconic, shimmering, gold leaf tiled pyramid atop the New York Life building. The 1928 Gilbert Cass design is also a National Historic Landmark and also designated locally by New York Landmarks Conservancy.

Across the terrace, in all its art deco glory, stands New York City's even more famous edifice, the Empire State Building (see ch. 43). If you look carefully, you can see a sliver of the enormous green roof installed in 2011 on the 21st-floor setback of this iconic structure. This 1931 symbol of New York City was retrofitted to be Manhattan's "greenest" building, with green roofs as just one of the upgrades that make this building more energy efficient than any other Gotham skyscraper.

Countless rooftop water towers, a few fading advertisements painted on the sides of buildings, an aging decorative cornice on the building next door, and the patchwork of old decorated towers next to new glass curtain wall construction makes the view from The Heights endlessly fascinating.

Address Arlo NoMad Hotel, 11 East 31st Street, 31st Floor, New York, NY 10016, +1 (212)951-1141, www.theheightsarlonomad.com | Getting there Subway to 34th Street–Herald Square (Line B, D, F, M, N, Q, R, W), or bus M1, M2, M3 to Madison Avenue/East 30th Street | Hours Mon–Wed 4pm–midnight, Thu–Sun noon–1am | Tip For a contrasting, street-level NYC experience, take the 8-minute walk to the 2nd Ave Deli for pastrami piled high on rye (162 East 33rd Street, New York, NY 10016, www.2ndavedeli.com).

53 — The High Line
Walk slowly and smell the flowers

Oreos have been among America's favorite cookies for over 100 years. For decades after they were invented in 1912, every Oreo that would satisfy the entire country's cravings for the cream-filled chocolate sandwich cookies was baked in the huge National Biscuit Company (Nabisco) factory on the West Side of Manhattan, and all the ingredients to make them were delivered by rail.

What remains of the railway that gave us Oreos, Fig Newtons, Saltines, and more is now the High Line. Just under 1.5 miles long, the High Line is an elevated garden, public park, and outdoor art gallery built on what remains of a once-busy freight rail line. From 1934 through the 1960s, continuous carloads of manufactured goods traveled in and out of Manhattan via what was then called the West Side Line. Particularly unique was that the tracks ran through buildings, making highly efficient stops inside the factories, dropping off and picking up goods exactly where they were needed.

As trucks replaced trains for delivering goods, the West Side Line became a disused, rusty eyesore. Most of the tracks below Gansevoort Street to the terminus at Spring Street were demolished before 1970, but the portion above Gansevoort Street continued service, though much less frequently, until 1980.

In 2001, Rudy Giuliani, just days before he left office as the mayor of New York City, ordered that the remaining 1.5 miles of the abandoned freight line be torn down. Fortunately, community action saved the structure.

Today, the High Line welcomes over six million visitors a year, and this once-neglected rail line has spurred the proliferation of luxury buildings by a who's who of top architects along its path. A park for strolling that winds through the urban experience, the High Line is an ever-changing, elevated garden that richly rewards repeat visits throughout the four seasons.

Address From Gansevoort and Washington Streets to West 34th Street and 12th Avenue, New York, +1 (212)500-6035, www.thehighline.org, info@thehighline.org | Getting there Subway to 14th Street (Line A, C, E), to 8th Avenue (Line L), or bus M 11 to Greenwich Street/Horatio Street | Hours See website for seasonal hours | Tip Chelsea Market in the former Nabisco factory is a food-lovers' paradise. Stroll through the block-long building, stopping to try foods from around the globe. Make sure to check out the basement-level shops too, and the Artists & Fleas Makers Market at the 10th Avenue entrance (75 Ninth Avenue, New York, NY 10011, www.chelseamarket.com, www.artistsandfleas.com).

54__ The Ides Bar

Skip to the front of the line, and no tipping

Built in a 1901 cooperage, The Ides Bar on the sixth floor of the trendy Wythe Hotel melds the historic with the modern on the Williamsburg waterfront. The first of several swanky rooftop bars in this corner of Brooklyn, The Ides remains one of the best. Devoted to a superb customer experience, The Ides continues to improve on its seasonal bar menu, revamp the spacious three-sided terrace, and limit guests at peak times so all who manage to get in can delight in the space as it is meant to be.

Getting in is a breeze: Reserve online, and same-day reservations are taken for spur-of-the-moment outings. Tell the hotel receptionists you have a reservation, and they will bring you to the front of the line for the next elevator to the sixth floor. Once there, enjoy a fabulous menu of expertly made classic cocktails and seasonally changing spirit-based concoctions, as well as local beers on tap and a selection of mostly French natural wines. Prices include a gratuity, so there is no need to tip, which makes going to The Ides feel almost like you're visiting a private club.

Indoors holds 80 people comfortably and is brimming with thoughtful details, such as bar hooks to keep your handbag off the floor and out of your lap. Shallow shelves around the perimeter of the pillars and along the walls let you park your drink while you socialize and enjoy the view behind the back bar. Music is kept in the background so you can converse. The Ides is least crowded during the week, when getting a quiet corner table or a seat at the beautiful marble bar is easiest.

In good weather, step out to the terrace, big enough to hold 100 more guests. Especially at sunset, take in the Manhattan skyline and Brooklyn views. An unusual perk for this hotel offering bunk bed rooms is that until 7 o'clock The Ides is family-friendly. But after that, it's just for the grownups.

Address Wythe Hotel, 80 Wythe Avenue, 6th Floor, Brooklyn, NY 11211, +1 (718)460-8006, www.wythehotel.com/the-ides | **Getting there** Subway to Bedford Avenue (Line L), or Nassau Avenue (Line G) | **Hours** Mon–Thu 4pm–close, Fri 2pm–close, Sat & Sun noon–close | **Tip** Take the NYC Ferry to get where you're going or simply to enjoy the views. For the same low price as a subway fare, you can take a tour of the East River or even out to catch the waves at Rockaway Beach (www.ferry.nyc).

55 Irish Hunger Memorial

A bit of rural Ireland in Lower Manhattan

Immerse yourself in a quarter-acre of the emerald isle on the living roof of the Irish Hunger Memorial, a thought-provoking homage to *An Gota Mór*, Gaelic for "The Great Hunger," but more commonly known as The Great Potato Famine. Between 1845 and 1852, nearly a million Irish people starved to death, and nearly another million emigrated to New York City in a desperate attempt to survive.

Artist Brian Tolle's multidimensional memorial leads visitors from the exterior path and through a tunnel made of 300-million-year-old Kilkenny limestone, black threaded with white fossils and extracted from the Irish seabed. The tunnel is filled with voices while ghostly backlit written texts offer heartbreaking details regarding the history of the Great Famine along with current reports on world hunger.

This passageway opens into a ruined Irish fieldstone cottage donated by relatives of the artist, the Slack family of County Mayo. Moving forward, visitors climb the gently sloping, 25-foot roof built on the limestone plinth and supported by 230,000 pounds of cantilever rebar. The plantings, designed by landscape architect Gail Wittwer-Laird, are comprised of 60 varieties of Irish flora. With foxglove, blackthorn, ling heather, and indigenous Irish grasses, it feels as if a bit of rural Ireland has landed on this sloping rooftop in Lower Manhattan. At the top of the path, visitors face West over the Hudson River and out toward the Statue of Liberty and Ellis Island, poignant reminders of the refuge sought by The Great Potato Famine survivors.

Scattered throughout the memorial are large engraved stones, one from each of Ireland's 32 counties. For help finding the rock representing your ancestor's county, some of which are indeed hard to find, download the free Irish Hunger Memorial app for a map and much more information about this unique, publicly accessible rooftop memorial.

Address Vesey Street at North End Avenue, New York, NY 10280, +1 (212)267-9700, www.bpcparks.org/whats-here/parks/irish-hunger-memorial | **Getting there** Subway to Cortland Street (Line 1), to World Trade Center (Line E), to Chambers Street (Line 1, 2, 3), or bus M20 to Vesey Street/North End Avenue | **Hours** Daily 8am–6pm | **Tip** Adjacent to the memorial is Brookfield Place, a high-end shopping destination with frequent free art exhibits and live performances, a food hall and restaurants, 40-plus posh shops, and a winter ice rink (230 Vesey Street, New York, NY 10281, www.brookfieldplaceny.com).

56 Jane Hotel Rooftop Bar

Once a beacon for sailors and Titanic *survivors*

Time travel to the New York City of more than a hundred years ago when the West Side was dotted with busy shipping piers, and merchant sailors on leave filled the dangerous and dingy streets. To keep those boys out of trouble, the American Seamen's Friend Society built what is now known as the Jane Hotel near the edge of the Hudson River. Tiny, cabin-like rooms were made for sailors used to tight spaces, and a light beacon anchored in the octagonal room on the sixth-floor rooftop served to warn ships that they were dangerously close to shore. Surviving *Titanic* crew members stayed here upon arriving on the *RMS Carpathia.*

Now a landmarked building, the beacon is long gone, but the octagonal rooftop room that held it has been reinvented as a charming lounge with Victorian velvet settees and a carved oak bar. Through the door with a porthole-shaped window is the roof terrace that holds no more than 40 guests.

Strings of dim bulbs and the brick parapet wall surround the low cushioned furniture where guests can easily have a conversation because the music is restricted to the indoor bar. The high stools next to the parapet wall allow for a view across one of the Hudson River Park playgrounds and the mighty river after which the park is named. The bar is a great place to watch ferries, cruise ships, kayaks, motor boats, and yachts on the Hudson.

This landmarked hotel, designed by William A. Boring, the architect most famous for Ellis Island's immigrant station, was lovingly restored in 2008, one hundred years after it was completed. When you feel the need for a little getaway from modern day New York City, the Jane Hotel Rooftop Bar is an ideal summertime choice. A quick word of advice: Call to make sure the roof is open when you want to go. It's no surprise that this little charmer of an old-time-style rooftop bar is frequently rented out for private events.

Address The Jane Hotel, 113 Jane Street, New York, NY 10014, +1 (212)924-6700, www.thejanenyc.com | **Getting there** Subway to 14th Street (Line A, C, E), to 8th Avenue (Line L), or bus M 11 to Greenwich Street / Horatio Street | **Hours** May–Sep, daily 5pm–2am, weather permitting | **Tip** For a raucous time aboard a floating restaurant, grab a drink aboard the *Frying Pan*, a permanently docked 1929 historic lightship (Pier 66 at Hudson River Park, West 26th Street, New York, NY 10001, www.fryingpan.com).

57 Javits Center Green Roof
The second largest green roof and bird sanctuary

In 1986, when Javits Center opened its doors, volunteers from the New York Audubon Society would count the number of dead bird carcasses around the base of the building that was aptly nicknamed "Darth Vader." More birds met their violent death by flying into the bird-confusing, black reflective Jacob K. Javits Convention Center than any other building in New York City.

More than 20 years and half a billion dollars later, the Javits Center is one of the most bird, bat, and bee-friendly buildings in the city. Today, the USA's busiest convention center's rooftop also has the country's second largest green roof, right after the Ford Motor Company's Rouge Center near Dearborn, Michigan. This seemingly endless, low-flung, sedum garden covers more area than five football fields.

Over 25 distinct bird species have been recorded nesting, resting, or feeding on Javits' vast living roof. A bat-sensitive microphone has recorded visits by five of the region's nine bat species. Five bee hives with more than 60,000 pollinating honey bees call this roof home. Solar panels collect energy, and two weather stations collect data. Even the condensation from the HVAC units is collected into tiny dishes that provide fresh water to the visiting birds. The reflective glass that used to confuse flying birds has been replaced with dotted glass that helps birds recognize a building to be avoided rather than a reflection of a flock to be joined. Since replacing 6,000 glass panels, bird deaths are down by 90%.

Nearly 100 nests have been established on Javits' roof, and scores of baby gulls have safely hatched in what is now a rooftop avian sanctuary. You can watch birds flying around and landing on the green roof from your smartphone via the live "Roof Cam," accessible on the Javits Center's website. But it's best to see it in person. Free tours fill up fast, so book early.

Address 655 West 34th Street, New York, NY 10001, +1 (212)216-2000, www.javitscenter.com, moreinfo@javitscenter.com | Getting there Subway to 34th Street–Hudson Yards (Line 7), bus M 34 to West 34th Street/12th Avenue, or bus M 12 to 11th Avenue/West 38th Street | Hours Tours Apr–Oct by appointment only | Tip A classic Irish pub, the Landmark Tavern has been serving New Yorkers comforting drinks and food since 1868, before 12th Avenue even existed. The tavern survived Prohibition by becoming a third-floor speakeasy for a time (626 Eleventh Avenue, New York, NY 10036, www.thelandmarktavern.com).

58_JIMMY

Splash the summer away at rooftop pool parties

There's no need to be a guest at The James Hotel in SoHo to take advantage of two very different outdoor, above-ground experiences offered by this super trendy hotel. The low-key and quieter option of the two rooftop experiences is to relax on or next to the patch of lawn in the charming, hidden grassy terrace two floors above Spring Street. The trick is to find it: head up the stairs *behind* the garden seating for David Burke Kitchen, and the serene little oasis awaits. Pick up a drink from the restaurant along the way if you'd like, as there is no service on this garden terrace.

If serene is not what you're looking for, and if you're willing to wait until 3 to 8pm on summer weekends, splashing in the pool next to the outdoor bar called JIMMY on the 18th floor is also available to those without room keys. Just remember to hit the gym regularly for six months before the summer season begins, don your best swimwear, pack your credit card for drinks and snacks, and make a reservation for some of downtown's most popular rooftop pool parties. If you've been a little lax with the workouts, you can still have fun at these parties. Wear smart-casual clothes and hang out ringside to watch the bathers cool off in the small pool with the iridescent tiles that is the true centerpiece of this trendy rooftop bar. Try a specialty cocktail, such as the Low Rider or the Ambassador Swizzle.

When it's not Summer Pool Party season, JIMMY's outdoor bar is less chaotic and open for a lively crowd taking advantage of the casual poolside atmosphere and the spectacular views. During winter, the lounge furniture is stored for the season, but the outdoor space remains open. And when New York City gets super frosty, the splash pool freezes over. That occasional phenomenon is definitely worth a quick look, but then you can retreat into JIMMY's indoor party and peer through the floor-to-ceiling windows for breathtaking views, including the World Trade Center.

Address The James Hotel, 15 Thompson Street, 18th Floor, NY 10013, www.jimmysoho.com, reservations@jimmysoho.com | Getting there Subway to Canal Street (Line 1, A, C, E), or bus M 55 to 6th Avenue/Thompson Street | Hours Mon–Wed 5pm–1am, Thu & Fri 5pm–2am, Sat 3pm–2am, Sun 3pm–1am | Tip The Jackie Robinson Museum is filled with memorabilia from the sports legend's life and baseball career. It also conveys a message to conquer barriers and resist bullies (75 Varick Street, New York, NY 10013, www.jackierobinson.org/museum).

59__Juliette

French cuisine with a Williamsburg twist

Since the borough's leading role in the hipster revolution, people around the world have fallen madly in love with Brooklyn. Tourists, mostly from Western Europe and Asia, flock to Williamsburg, the trend's epicenter, in droves. Any French national walking down North 5th Street between Bedford and Berry can't help but notice three flags – the tri-colored French flag, the fleur-de-lis, and the black-and-white striped flag of Brittany – waving from the roof of a midblock bistro, clearly indicating that this is a bit of home away from home. Many of the staff speak French and, not surprisingly, the establishment is owned by an expat from Brittany, who named the restaurant after his daughter Juliette.

Tourists traveling across the waters from France, Japan, and Manhattan mingle with Brooklynites on the popular rooftop at Juliette. There are even frequent celebrity sightings, so keep your eyes peeled for familiar faces from TV, movies, and music.

Not that long ago, before Williamsburg was the symbol of all things hipster, it was a working-class neighborhood, so it's no surprise that Juliette's cozy downstairs seating used to be a car repair garage. Off to the side, the winter garden room with the skylight ceiling and jungle of hanging plants, was formerly the neighboring property's backyard. The rooftop restaurant and bar, with its colorful seating and charming umbrellas, was created after the transformation from garage to bistro by the resourceful owner who fashioned an unrushed place to enjoy excellent French-inspired food, well-made cocktails, and local beers on tap.

Williamsburg likes to sleep late on the weekends, so the best time to get a rooftop table or seat at the bar is between 10:30am and noon on Saturdays and Sundays. After that, there may be a wait for a rooftop seat, even if you made a reservation, although that will speed things along a bit.

Address 135 North 5th Street, Brooklyn, NY 11249, +1 (718)388-9222, www.juliettewilliamsburg.com, info@juliettewilliamsburg.com | **Getting there** Subway to Bedford Avenue (Line L), to Metropolitan Avenue (Line G), or bus B 62 to Bedford Avenue/North 8th Street | **Hours** Mon–Fri 10:30am–11pm, Sat & Sun 10:30am–4pm & 5pm–midnight | **Tip** Experience of-the-moment, creative live music in the magical venue called National Sawdust (80 North 6th Street, Brooklyn, NY 11249, www.nationalsawdust.org).

60 Kids Clubhouse
Yankee Stadium fun for the littlest baseball fans

A family outing to Yankee Stadium to see the 27-time world champion, pinstripe-clad, Bronx Bombers seems like a great idea – that is, until your preschool-age child starts squirming in his or her seat. In 2017, Yankee Stadium designers took their littlest fans' needs to heart and built a Yankee-themed kids' zone specifically designed for those under three-and-a-half feet tall, though slightly taller siblings can join in the fun.

Situated on the roof terrace above the Yankees Museum, the 2,850-square-foot safe place for kids to play is all things Yankees: a baseball diamond-shaped area holds a climbable, oversized ball cap encrusted with the famous New York Yankees logo, a giant bat and ball, a catcher's mitt, baseball cards, bases, a hotdog, and a mound of peanuts. A Yankees pennant works as a mini slide and, of course, there is a six-foot-tall replica of a World Series trophy, big enough for kids to play hide and seek inside. An older sibling might want to try pitching a Wiffle ball into the strike zone. Parents hang out in the dugouts where they can watch the game on TV. Nursing moms are afforded private rooms with lounge chairs, and two family-friendly restrooms make sure potty accidents can be easily avoided. The colorful playground is on a roof terrace, so be sure to notice the view facing south toward the clearly recognizable, jagged Manhattan skyline.

Once fans have gained entry to the park, admission to the Kids Clubhouse is free, with the strict caveat that adults can only enter if they are accompanying a child. This Clubhouse opens when Yankee Stadium's gates are lifted and stays open through the end of the 7th inning. Letting the kids run off some of their boundless energy before settling them in their seats for the first pitch or giving them a mid-game play break might just make your trek to Yankee Stadium the perfect family day out.

Address Adjacent to section 310 in Yankee Stadium, 1 East 161st Street, Bronx, NY 10451, +1 (212)926-5337, https://www.mlb.com/yankees/ballpark | **Getting there** Subway to 161st Street–Yankee Stadium (Line 4, B, D), bus Bx6 to East 161st Street/Macombs Dam Bridge, or bus Bx13 to E 161st Street/River Avenue | **Hours** On game days when gates open until end of the 7th inning | **Tip** Monument Park, located inside Yankee Stadium at field level, honors ballplayers and other notables associated with Yankees history (www.mlb.com/yankees/ballpark/information/guide).

61 Kimoto Rooftop Garden Lounge

Asian libations on a Brooklyn rooftop

Kimoto is a Japanese word describing a variation on the brewing method that lends the sake a gamier, wilder flavor. It is also the name of the rooftop bar in downtown Brooklyn that, from 24 floors up, has views across the most populated New York City borough, out as far as the Verrazano Bridge, and even offers a distant glimpse of the Statue of Liberty in New York Harbor.

While much of Kimoto is covered for year-round comfort, there is a completely open-air corner from which you see the spectacular Brooklyn vista described above. You are not in Manhattan, and you are not looking toward the mass of skyscrapers blanketing the island borough, but all the high-rise construction going on around Kimoto might make any native Brooklynite wonder exactly where, in fact, they are. There are so many cranes, workers in hard hats, and new and under-construction skyscrapers, it is just about unrecognizable. Several of the surrounding new buildings have private rooftops for residents, but from the 24th floor, you can peer into their creative use of rooftop space.

Kimoto focuses on Asian cocktails, including sake and shochu, as well as a large selection of New York and Asian craft beers. A rooftop lunch and dinner restaurant featuring beautifully prepared Japanese fare is served on an indoor terrace that opens to the outside. The outdoor patio is reserved for cocktails and small bites, which are served until the wee hours, especially on Friday and Saturday nights when a DJ and terrific lighting create a rooftop party atmosphere.

Kimoto is popular for private events, so it is prudent to confirm that the rooftop is open to the public when you're looking for the unique combination of an Asian party atmosphere with long-reaching Brooklyn views.

Address Aloft Hotel, 216 Duffield Street, 24th Floor, Brooklyn, NY 11201, +1 (718)858-8940, www.kimotorooftop.com, info@kimotorooftop.com | **Getting there** Subway to Jay Street–MetroTech (Line A, F, N, R, W), or bus B 25, B 26, B 38, B 52 to Fulton Street / Duffield Street | **Hours** Sun–Wed noon–midnight, Thu–Sat noon–close | **Tip** Hungry? Try some of the 40 dazzling food vendors at the DeKalb Market Hall across the street in the sprawling basement at City Point (445 Albee Square West, Brooklyn, NY 11201, www.dekalbmarkethall.com).

62 Kingsland Wildflowers at Broadway Stages

Nature returns to Newtown Creek one roof at a time

Starting in the 1840s, scores of oil refineries opened next to Newtown Creek. Over time, an estimated 30 million gallons of crude oil leaked into the creek and surrounding areas, making Greenpoint, Brooklyn home to the largest underground oil spill to occur in the United States.

Kingsland Wildflowers, one of the beneficiaries of recovery funding, is an educational and science-focused green roof fostering ecology, sustainability, and community. Originally envisioned in 2015 by local landscape designer Marni Majorelle of Alive Structures, in partnership with New York City Audubon and Newtown Creek Alliance, the project was financed by the Greenpoint Community Environmental Fund and Broadway Stages. Together they decided to build a series of green roofs primarily using native plants, thus creating a green corridor for flora and fauna. New York City Audubon urban wildlife and ecology experts monitor the green roof habitat that draws back native bird, bat, and insect populations.

In 2016, 10,000 square feet of native plants took root on the rooftop of one of Broadway Stages' Greenpoint sound stages. A field of flowers now thrives a few stories above the oil spill site. A year later, an additional 12,000 square feet of native plants and sedum were installed on two other roof elevations of this enormous structure. A fifth green roof, donated by Broadway Stages and dedicated to environmental education, brings the total green roof space to over half an acre.

Three of the five green roofs are accessible by the public. Two inaccessible sedum roofs on lower elevations act as a magnet for a myriad of native pollinators. Careful rooftop planning and planting are helping to recreate and restore the environment next to what was once a major environmental disaster.

Address 520 Kingsland Avenue, Brooklyn, NY 11222, www.kingslandwildflowers.com, info@kingslandwildflowers.com | **Getting there** Subway to Greenpoint Avenue (Line G), or bus B 24 to Greenpoint Avenue / Kingsland Avenue | **Hours** Seasonally Apr–Nov; check events page on website | **Tip** Next door is the Newtown Creek Nature Walk, a quarter-mile trail of native trees, shrubs, and other flora along Newtown Creek and Whale Creek (www.nyc.gov/html/dep/html/environmental_education/newtown).

63 __ Laurie M. Tisch Illumination Lawn

Catch a breeze on Lincoln Center's warping parabola

One of only a handful of public-access roof lawns in the city, the sloping turf of the Laurie M. Tisch Illumination Lawn at Lincoln Center, even on the hottest days, is the ideal place to enjoy an Upper West Side breeze and take a load off your weary feet. Muse over the Henry Moore sculpture, *Reclining Figure*, in the adjacent reflecting pool, take a picnic, or take a nap, all excellent ways to enjoy this urban lawn in the sky.

This green roof, in the highly original shape of a large warping parabola, caps the lauded Lincoln Ristorante and the Elinor Bunin Munroe Film Center. The pointed exterior of the recently renovated Alice Tully Hall across West 65th Street echoes the point of this rooftop parabola. Designed by the team who created the High Line (see ch. 53), Diller Scofidio + Renfro, the 7,200-square-foot Illumination Lawn has easy access via built-in steps at its base so climbing onto this particular rooftop is always perfectly safe.

Free and centrally located, this living roof is popular during good weather and sometimes needs a rest from visitors to rejuvenate, so access is restricted from time to time. But year-round, it is a feast for the eyes.

Hidden green roofs abound at Lincoln Center. When at the Illumination Lawn, take a moment to notice two less-obvious ones. The adjacent Barclay Capital Grove was planted using green roof technology, similar to the National September 11 Memorial in Lower Manhattan. Those perfect rows of London Plane trees may appear to be planted in ground, but they are, in fact, in containers under the plaza's surface. Another hidden green roof is at the Claire Tow Theater, a 112-seat experimental playhouse built atop the Beaumont. It sports a handsome green roof surrounding its outdoor deck.

Address West 65th Street between Broadway and Amsterdam, New York, NY 10023,
www.lincolncenter.org/venue/hearst-plaza | Getting there Subway to 66th Street–Lincoln
Center (Line 1) | Hours Unrestricted except during lawn rejuvenation | Tip Get a $30
ticket to see an experimental play in the Claire Tow Theater (150 West 65th Street,
New York, NY 10023, www.lct.org/about/claire-tow-theater), but make sure to go an hour
before curtain when the large outdoor deck built just above a green roof offers a spectacular
view of Lincoln Center and the Juilliard campus across the street.

64__Leaf Bar & Lounge

Try the rooftop bar at the end of the line

We all ride the New York City subways, but it's not often that we remain on board until the end of the line. When you stay on the 7 line until the very last stop, you emerge from the underground terminus to a lively Queens neighborhood more closely resembling Hong Kong or mainland China. Stores display signs in Chinese and sell everything from Asian groceries to Chinese herbal medicines to Shanghai's latest pop hits. This hectic Chinatown is home to a burgeoning blue-collar immigrant population and receives a significant influx from Chinese investors that funds a veritable building boom.

Just one of many new structures is home to the only rooftop bar in Flushing. Ten stories up, with views over Citi Field, Flushing Creek, and the distant Manhattan skyline, the trendy Leaf Bar & Lounge offers guests its own take on Asian Fusion. While the décor is decidedly American, with an unfinished wood-clad bar and a flat-screen TV showing the big games, the menu gives plenty of nods to Far Eastern cultures with cocktail ingredients including shochu, sake, and even chrysanthemum-infused bourbon. The bar offers a seasonal and signature list of creative and delicious libations. Try a Hellcat or a Gone Guavas.

In Leaf's kitchen are two brothers from Taiwan – with a several-year stopover in Bolivia, oddly enough – who cook a traditional Taiwanese beef noodle soup. Regulars call it the best in Queens and come back often for this homemade delicacy. The brothers also make an Asian-American mashup that perfectly suits the vibe – cheeseburger spring rolls. Salt & pepper popcorn chicken remains a perennial favorite while lounging on one of the two open-air roof decks, or when it's colder, inside the spacious bar.

Consider taking an entire afternoon for your next New York City roof adventure. Ride the 7 train as far east as it goes to Flushing's Main Street. You'll discover many earthly delights of the Asian continent and the airy pleasures of this chic rooftop bar.

Address Hyatt Place Rooftop, 133-42 39th Avenue, Queens, NY 11354, +1 (718)865-8158, www.leafbarandlounge.com, info@leafbarandlounge.com | Getting there Subway to Flushing–Main Street (Line 7), or bus Q12, Q15, Q26 to Flushing Main Street | Hours Mon–Thu 5pm–1am, Fri & Sat 5pm–2am, Sun 5pm–midnight | Tip For a wild ride to all three of New York City's Chinatowns in Manhattan, Brooklyn, and Queens, take the Zhong Hua (Chinatown Small Buses) shuttle. It's uncomfortable, cheap, and won't leave until the bus is full, but it will take you on an amazing journey of discovery (Division Street & Bowery, New York, NY 10002, www.explorechinatown.com).

65 LeFrak Center at Lakeside

Meander through a one-acre rooftop woodland

Hasidic boys with short hair and long side locks zipping along on their scooters, an elderly couple with canes sauntering amongst the blossoming trees, and an oversized hound dog tethered on an extended leash bringing the ball back to his master. All this and more happens on the winding pathways of the LeFrak Center at Lakeside's green roof.

The building next to the skating rink was cleverly built into the sloping earth, making the roof of the café and offices housed there feel like a natural extension of the park. On the other side of this elevated garden, the rental lockers adjacent to the rink are below the living roof, and the two rooftops are connected by a wooden slat bridge like a miniature version of a beach boardwalk.

This enormous, L-shaped green roof, built solidly enough to support dozens of large trees, seamlessly integrates into the surrounding landscape of this southeast corner of Prospect Park. The gently sloping paved paths that lead through these connected rooftops start on the long side of the L, and near the bike rental kiosk on the shorter side, making this $74-million capital improvement to Prospect Park accessible to the diverse urban community surrounding it.

Reaching 23 feet in height, this green roof sets up bucolic views of the beloved park designed by Olmsted and Vaux that was completed in 1874, a few years after this famous team of landscape designers finished Central Park in Manhattan. The contemporary music from the roller rink and splash pool during summer and ice-skating rink during winter belies the visual trip back in time to the 19th century. On both sides of the rooftop, the paths lead to large terraces that overlook the covered portion of the rink for a very 21st-century experience, complete with a view of the regulation hockey-size pad and skating music emanating from an array of speakers.

Address Prospect Park, 171 East Drive, Brooklyn, NY 11225, www.lakesidebrooklyn.com | Getting there Subway to Prospect Park (Line B, Q), to Parkside Avenue (Line Q), to Grand Army Plaza (Line 2, 3) to 15 Street/Prospect Park or Fort Hamilton Parkway (Line F, G), bus B 12 to Parkside Avenue/Ocean Avenue, bus B 41 to Grand Army Plaza, bus B 48 to Lincoln Road, bus B 68 to Park Circle, bus B 16 to Ocean Avenue/Parkside Avenue, or bus B 41 to Woodruff Avenue/Flatbush Avenue | Hours Daily 5 – 1am | Tip Pull out your 70s' dance party clothes and rent some skates each Friday night during the summer months for the weekly roller-disco parties (171 East Drive, Brooklyn, NY 11225, www.lakesidebrooklyn.com/activities).

66 Liberty Park

Remembering 9/11 and looking to the future

Atop the parking garage that services the World Trade Center complex is Liberty Park, with lush trees and shrub gardens. Look for a particularly symbolic tree, a sapling grown from the chestnut tree that was Anne Frank's only view of the outside world while she and her family hid for 25 months until being found by the Nazis. Nearby, in the southwest corner of this park, is *The Horse Soldier*, a statue commemorating US troops that fought in Afghanistan. You will also see *The Sphere*, a globelike sculpture by artist Fritz Koenig that once graced the World Trade Center Plaza. Its deep scars from September 11, 2001 reflect the events of that day.

Amphitheater-style seating at the Greenwich Street entrance and plenty of benches invite endlessly entertaining people-watching. Situated 25 feet above Liberty Street, Liberty Park is flanked by the West Side Highway to the west and Greenwich Street to the east. It was designed with two access points from street level: a wider staircase near Greenwich Street and a narrower one near West Street. The park can also be accessed via gently sloping ramps.

The north-facing façade of this structure hosts an enormous living wall, 336 feet long and 25 feet high. More than 22,000 plants embellish the entrance to the parking structure. At the east end of the park stands a spectacular Greek Orthodox church and non-denominational bereavement center designed by the Spanish "starchitect" Santiago Calatrava, who also designed the nearby Oculus, the striking structure that serves as a transit hub. Called The St. Nicholas National Shrine, this glow-in-the-dark structure with opaque walls replaces the Greek Orthodox church destroyed when the South Tower collapsed.

Views from Liberty Park include vistas of the National September 11 Memorial reflecting pools and the World Trade Center grounds. The park is open daily until 11pm and offers illuminated views of the sacred ground where the Twin Towers once stood.

Address Liberty Street between Greenwich Street and West Street, New York, NY 10006, +1 (212)435-7000, www.panynj.gov | Getting there Subway to Fulton Street (Line 2, 3, 4, 5, A, C, J, Z) | Hours Daily 6am–11pm | Tip Take the Liberty Street pedestrian bridge across West Street right into the high-fashion Brookfield Place shopping center, anchored by New York City's newest Saks Fifth Avenue department store. Hudson Eats, Brookfield Place's swanky food court, and Eataly offer numerous tempting options for creating your own Liberty Park picnic (230 Vesey Street, New York, NY 10281, www.bfplny.com).

67 __ Llama Inn

This place is a neighborhood secret, so shhh!

Dishes with origins in Peru, ceviche (raw fish cured in lemon), and quinoa (the ancient "super grain" that's really a seed) are familiar to many New Yorkers. A pisco sour is a well-known cocktail made from Peruvian white brandy. The Llama Inn, a Peruvian-inspired restaurant in Brooklyn, takes an even deeper dive into South American-influenced cuisine with beef heart, snappy sauces, whole roasted branzino, and a complex cocktail menu.

If Brooklyn is the borough where the trendiest food scene in New York City is currently happening, then Williamsburg is one of the scene's rock stars. However, Brooklyn's foodies, people with a particular interest in the latest edible adventure, are keeping Llama Inn a local secret.

Llama Inn is easy to keep hidden. It's built on an odd triangle next to the low rumble of the Brooklyn-Queens Expressway (BQE) at the "other end" of Williamsburg, closer to the Lorimer Street subway station than to the busier stop at Bedford Avenue. A gas station used to be on this corner, but since 2015, it's been mining chef Eric Ramirez's Peruvian heritage at this South American-inspired restaurant and bar.

Upstairs at Llama Inn is a cozy rooftop that seats only about 35, including the four stools at the outdoor bar. The whole menu is served on the roof, or you can get one of Llama Inn's cocktails based on *pisco* (clear Peruvian brandy) or *chicha morada* (a purple corn drink) with *anticuchos* (skewers) to nibble on.

A climbing grape vine and lush plants, hand-woven wall art, and Peruvian ceramics decorate this trendy rooftop. With a couple of umbrellas and some sail cloth strung overhead, much of the roof is exposed to the elements, so it's open only in good weather for as many months as it's warm enough to be enjoyed. Llama Inn offers blankets to guests if it's cooler, but the roof is closed in rainy weather.

Address 50 Withers Street, Brooklyn, NY 11211, +1 (718)387-3434, www.llamainnnyc.com, info@llamainnnyc.com | **Getting there** Subway to Lorimer Street (Line L), to Metropolitan Avenue (Line G), or bus B 48 to Lorimer Street / Meeker Avenue | **Hours** Dinner: Sun–Wed 5:30–10pm, Thu–Sat 5:30–11pm; brunch: Sat & Sun 10:30am–3pm | **Tip** Farm-fresh veggies, live music, food education, and cooking demonstrations happen every Saturday at McCarren Park Greenmarket (North 12th Street and Union Street, www.grownyc.org/greenmarket/brooklyn/greenpoint-sa, Sat 8am–3pm).

68 Loopy Doopy Rooftop Bar
Countless ice pop cocktails served

If awards were given for cocktail creativity, the genius who dreamed up the Prosecco & Ice Pop delight that is the signature drink at Loopy Doopy at the Conrad Hotel deserves a gold star. This intimate rooftop terrace seats only about 75 and fills up fast with grown-ups who still enjoy one of childhood's summer delights, a fruity ice pop, served stick side up in a Bordeaux wine glass with a choice of rosé or sparkling wine.

Perhaps this cocktail and the other tempting libations were inspired by the artwork after which this bar is named: *Loopy Doopy* by Sol LeWitt. The enormous purple and blue painting is near the hotel entrance below, and is one of the most notable pieces in a lobby filled with significant contemporary works of art.

The outdoor terrace at Loopy Doopy is kept comfortable from April until November because of the cleverly designed awnings that protect you from the sun during the daytime and keep you warm in the evenings with their stylish built-in heat lamps. No reservations are taken at Loopy Doopy, so arrive well before dusk at this drinks-only bar if you want to catch the spectacular sunset.

If it weren't for the unmistakable views of the Hudson River, New York Harbor, and down toward Lady Liberty, you might not even be certain that you're in New York City. The Battery Park City buildings surrounding Loopy Doopy were constructed within the last few decades and are all LEED-certified with old New York City nowhere in sight! In fact, Battery Park City did not exist until 1976 when the land reclamation project on which it is built was completed. Before then, this part of Manhattan was, in fact, not Manhattan at all, but part of the Hudson River. When the Twin Towers were being erected in the late 1960s, workers dug so deeply into the city's bedrock that enough debris was excavated to create the entirely new neighborhood of Battery Park City.

Address Conrad Hotel, 102 North End Avenue, 16th Floor, New York, NY 10282, +1 (646)769-4250, www.conradnewyork.com/dine/loopy-doopy-rooftop-bar, LoopyDoopy.Bar@ConradHotels.com | **Getting there** Subway to Cortland Street (Line 1), to Chambers Street (Line 1, 2, 3), to World Trade Center (Line E), or bus M 20 to Vesey Street / North End Avenue | **Hours** Apr – Nov, daily 2 – 10pm | **Tip** Permanent, outdoor ping-pong and billiards tables are available just north of Loopy Doopy along the river's edge in Rockefeller Park. The Parkhouse loans games and equipment every day from May through October (75 Battery Place, New York, NY 10280, www.bpcparks.org/whats-here/parks/rockefeller-park).

69 The Lotus Garden

A secret oasis salvaged from the rubble

Possibly the oldest and certainly one of the most unusual community gardens in Manhattan is tucked away on top of a nondescript parking garage with access only through a large metal gate in front of a foreboding concrete staircase. Yet those bold enough to enter are rewarded with a lush, serene hideaway called The Lotus Garden.

Twenty-eight individual plots and two fish ponds surrounded by meandering pathways seamlessly meld together to create a spectacular micro-park that spans a cozy one-sixth of an acre. This unexpected retreat is filled with an artful collection of plants: a peach tree, hostas, lilies, astilbes, flowering shrubs and bushes, an herb garden, and a rock garden with alpine plants. This beloved garden is also adorned with statuary, benches, tables, and chairs inviting New Yorkers to instantly feel calmer in this peaceful, nature-filled environment.

In 1912, two ornate vaudeville theaters that became movie palaces adorned this then-suburban street, far from the densely populated neighborhoods in Lower Manhattan. But the theaters met their demise with the wrecking ball in 1976, leaving an acre of rubble that neighbors turned into a community garden. In 1984, when the land was eventually developed, the gardeners were granted one-sixth of an acre on top of a reinforced parking garage that was engineered to hold two-and-a-half feet of rain-saturated soil and plants. The Lotus Garden was born.

A true community hub, there are annual summer solstice celebrations and Halloween costume contests held at The Lotus Garden. For a nominal fee, Upper West Side residents can purchase a key to enter the garden during daylight hours for a semi-private, safe sanctuary above the hustle and bustle, and the general public is welcomed in to enjoy this bit of heaven each Sunday afternoon during the warmer months of the year when the garden is being lovingly tended.

Address West 97th Street between Broadway and West End Avenue, New York,
NY 10025, www.thelotusgarden.org | Getting there Subway to 96th Street (Line 1, 2, 3) |
Hours Apr–Nov, Sun 1–4pm | Tip Two blocks away from the Lotus Garden, between
Broadway and West End Avenue and 94th and 95th Streets, is arguably the cutest street in
Manhattan, Pomander Walk. This gated, secret street filled with tiny Tudor-style houses
was built in 1927. The houses were only meant to stay up for a few years, but Pomander
Walk survived and, in 1982, it was granted New York City Landmark status.

70__Luna Asian Bistro

Multicultural rooftop sushi and cocktails

Astoria, a longtime destination for authentic Greek fare, is becoming much more than that. The area's relative affordability and easy subway access is attracting a new crowd. A ferry stop makes traveling from Astoria to Brooklyn and Manhattan a joy, and new housing is under construction. Trendy clubs, bars, beloved brunch spots, a plethora of ethnic restaurants, shops, and close-by museums add to Astoria's allure. It is one of the fastest gentrifying and most culturally diverse neighborhoods in the five boroughs.

It's no surprise, then, that Luna is the Spanish name chosen by a Chinese owner and sushi chef for his Japanese restaurant. This multicultural mashup could only happen in Queens, where people from around the world live side-by-side, wanting, literally, to taste other cultures.

It's easy to miss Luna's midblock entrance in an office building. The lobby elevator will whisk you to the sixth-floor sushi bar, lounge, and fine-dining establishment that has two levels of outdoor space. On the sixth floor, look further into Queens, and on the seventh-floor terrace, see across the East River toward Manhattan. The East River breeze is a refreshing delight during the summer, but a frigid blast on winter nights. That's why the two transparent igloos set up for wintertime rooftop dining are both on the Queens-facing rooftop; when erected on the Manhattan-facing terrace, they nearly blew away!

Affordable and beautiful sushi, sashimi, teriyaki, and tempura are on the extensive menu. Cocktails feature Asian ingredients but also include Mexican and Caribbean-inspired flavors. All can be enjoyed inside or outside on lounge furniture or at bistro tables all summer long. When it gets colder, reserve an igloo to dine under the night sky at this Japanese rooftop restaurant and lounge called by the Spanish word for what you'll see here on a clear night: *la luna*, the moon.

Address 32–72 Steinway Street, Astoria, NY 11103, +1 (917)832-7911, www.lunaasianbistro.com | **Getting there** Subway to Steinway Street (Line M, R), or bus Q 101 to Steinway Street/34th Avenue | **Hours** Mon–Fri 5pm–1am, Sat & Sun 12:30pm–1am | **Tip** Stunning indoor and outdoor art galleries in a former industrial building make The Noguchi Museum well worth the 1.3-mile walk (free admission on the first Friday of each month, closed Mon & Tue, 9-01 33rd Road, Queens, NY 11106, www.noguchi.org).

71 Magic Hour
You're never too old to love the circus

The circus was in town and anything was possible. Enormous-eared elephants in rhinestones balanced on their back legs, scantily clad trapeze artists in shimmering costumes flew through the air, and everything smelled of sticky, pink cotton candy. At Magic Hour Rooftop Bar & Lounge, a sprawling 18th-floor venue in Manhattan's Garment District, the circus and amusement park theme continues throughout Magic Hour's three bars, but this party has a sexy-bordering-on-kinky amusement park vibe designed specifically for over-21s.

It's a raucous, good time at Magic Hour Rooftop Bar & Lounge. The revolving carousel where revelers can lounge with cocktails is near Foreplay, the four-hole putt-putt course, where hot pink, over-sized, and oversexed decorative animals pose as if they are up for any sort of swinging party. Balloon-shaped light fixtures hang over the bar that is backed with funhouse mirrors where colorful cocktails are created. In fact, most everything at Magic Hour is vivid and photo-ready, including the guests who pose for selfies or group pictures everywhere, but especially from the edge of Foreplay where a clear view of the Empire State Building adorns each snapshot.

Every Thursday night, circus parties and Sunday afternoon bubble events ramp up the adult theme-park concept with entertainers and party favors. Sunday brunch is the only time under-21s are allowed in to Magic Hour to indulge in the rich, gooey, maple cotton candy served with the giant stack of pancakes or crispy French toast made with caramelized apples and maple syrup.

Certain areas of Magic Hour are open air, but much of the 8,000-square-foot venue is never exposed to the elements. During winter, all of Magic Hour is covered and cozy, making it a year-round party destination. Reservations are recommended, especially for the Thursday night and Sunday afternoon parties and brunch.

Where the Magic happens

Address Moxy Times Square, 485 Seventh Avenue, 18th Floor, New York, NY 10018, +1 (212)268-0188, www.magichourny.com | **Getting there** Subway to 34th Street – Herald Square (Line B, D, F, M, N, Q, R, W), to 34th Street – Penn Station (Line 1, 2, 3, A, C, E), bus M 4 to 7th Avenue/West 36th Street, or bus M 7, M 20 to 7th Avenue/West 37th Street | **Hours** Mon – Sat 4pm – late, Sun 9pm – 4am, brunch: Sat & Sun 11:30am – 3:30pm | **Tip** The Houdini Museum is truly a hidden gem. This tiny exhibition space located on the 4th floor of a nondescript office building in the Garment District, is home to an impressive collection of Harry Houdini memorabilia and also a well-stocked magic shop (213 West 35th Street, Suite 401, New York, NY 10001, www.houdinimuseumny.com).

72__Make Believe

For the picture-perfect selfie, drink here!

Make Believe at the Sixty LES Hotel, with its Gucci panther head wallpaper and eye-popping pink floral décor, was designed for guests to live out their fantasies. Make believe you are anyone you want to be: a glamorous pop star, an heiress, or perhaps an athlete. Everything is photographable, designed with selfies in mind, and the customers, it seems, are never more than a thumb's distance from their smartphones.

Most of Make Believe is indoors, but it is bookended by two outdoor terraces. While the small, south-facing roof allows smoking, the larger north-facing space has a photo-ready backdrop that includes the Empire State and the Chrysler Buildings.

Two 20-something guys who love New York City nightlife created Make Believe, aiming to make their venue female-friendly. They surmised that when Make Believe attracts women, men will follow, and the formula has been working just as planned. The inviting, deep pink velvet banquets, the bright pink pay phones that don't actually make calls but are great props, the oversized portrait of a fluffy lap dog, and the attentive and attractive all-male bar staff make it a fun place for groups of young women to meet for celebrations.

Less raucous than a nightclub, but more of a party atmosphere than a bar, Make Believe falls into the category that its proprietors call a "social club." While this 7th-floor club does not require membership, it is best suited for trend-and-body-conscious 20-somethings with some extra money to spend on their nights out. With this demographic in mind, the unique cocktail menu appeals to health-aware partygoers, featuring ingredients such as super-caffeinated matcha, as well as CBD, a legal, non-psychoactive oil derived from cannabis. Though CBD has not been proven to induce relaxation, at Make Believe, all you have to do to make it work for you is, well, make believe.

Address SIXTY LES, 190 Allen Street, 7th Floor, New York, NY 10002, +1 (212)542-8696, www.sixtyhotels.com/lower-east-side/eat-drink, hello@makebelievesixty.com | **Getting there** Subway to Second Avenue (Line F), or bus M 15 to Allen Street / Stanton Street | **Hours** Mon–Fri 6pm–late, Sat & Sun 2pm–late | **Tip** Russ & Daughters has sold high-quality smoked salmon, caviar, and baked goods in the same location since 1914 (179 East Houston Street, New York, NY 10002, www.shop.russanddaughters.com).

73 The Meyerson Family Roof Terrace

Everyone is welcome on JCC Manhattan's accessible rooftop

"If you build it, they will come," made famous by the 1989 movie, *Field of Dreams*, was about building a baseball stadium. The Marlene Meyerson JCC Manhattan's rooftop was created with a similar principle in mind. The JCC built a spacious, easily accessible, flexible, and safe open-air rooftop. Year-round, the Meyerson Family Roof Terrace has become the second-most popular public space in the entire 14-story community center.

Even after a winter storm, the rooftop offers a unique play space. Kids love to experience fresh, white snow. They want to ball it up and throw it, build with it, jump and roll around in it, and eat it. Finding clean snow in New York City is not easy, but what falls on this 3,000-plus-square-foot rooftop remains safe and clean. After all, it's nine floors above where anyone walks their dog!

On the other 300-plus days a year, the Meyerson Family Roof Terrace might be used for concerts, movies, Shabbat dinners, holiday celebrations, dances, camp, nursery school, and dozens of other activities that the bustling JCC Manhattan schedules. With programming designed to serve newborns to centenarians through each stage of life, the JCC Manhattan is a true community center.

The elevator delivers rooftop visitors to an indoor vestibule adjacent to the bathroom – they thought of everything! Stairs or a wheelchair-friendly ramp leads to the outside. The glass parapet is high, with views toward Central Park, located just two avenues away. Containers growing tomatoes, cucumbers, mint, basil, and even seven-foot-tall sunflowers are planted around the perimeter. Curvy benches and a kids' play gym are the only other permanent structures. The remaining open space easily accommodates 300-plus.

Address 334 Amsterdam Avenue, New York, NY 10023, +1 (646)505-4444, www.jccmanhattan.org, info@jccmanhattan.org | Getting there Subway to 72nd Street (Line 1, 2, 3, B, C), or bus M 7, M 11 to Amsterdam Avenue / West 75th Street | Hours Rooftop playground school days 3:30pm–dusk, camp days 2pm–dusk, non-school/camp weekdays 9am–4pm, Sat & Sun 7am–dusk, building: Mon–Thu 5:30am–11pm, Fri 5:30am–10pm, Sat & Sun 7am–10pm | Tip Zabar's is the Upper West Side's gourmet grocery mecca specializing in smoked fish, coffee, and cheese (2245 Broadway, New York, NY 10024, www.zabars.com).

74 Midtown Tennis Club
Where to find a tennis club hidden under a bubble

In 1965, Robert F. Wagner, the three-term conservative New York City mayor, lost to the liberal John Lindsay. Penn Station had recently been destroyed, spurring the creation of the Landmarks Preservation Commission. The Brooklyn Navy Yard launched its last Navy ship, Bob Dylan went electric, and Billie Jean King played on grass courts at the US National Championships in Flushing, now known as the US Open.

In that same year, over half a century ago, Midtown Tennis Club opened, with four indoor and four rooftop Har-Tru clay courts. From June 15 to September 15 each year, the protective rooftop bubble comes down for outdoor matches in the fresh air and sunshine. Four stories up, the courts are high enough above street noise to focus on the game, though the fabulous views that include the Empire State Building and the new skyscrapers emerging at Hudson Yards could prove distracting.

All are welcome at Midtown Tennis, where rooftop courts are easy to reserve. A membership option is offered but not required. With something for everyone, Midtown Tennis has a fun and affordable rooftop clinic for adult beginners each night all summer that continues on weekend evenings after the protective rooftop bubble goes up. A juniors program offers a summer kids' tennis camp and after-school classes the rest of the year. There is even a discounted outdoor tennis court membership special each summer.

Nestled midblock next to a dry cleaner, the easy-to-miss entrance hides what lies beyond, a low-key, beloved tennis mecca that has served many of the same New Yorkers for decades. A long-time member who is nearly 90 continues his regular game twice weekly. Celebrities are often seen at Midtown Tennis playing a match or two, and no one makes a fuss. Regardless of outside accomplishments, everyone is the same at Midtown Tennis Club. All are here because they love the game.

Address 341 Eighth Avenue, New York, NY 10001, +1 (212)989-8572,
www.midtowntennis.com, midtowntennisnyc@gmail.com | Getting there Subway to
23rd Street (Line C, E) | Hours Mon–Fri 7am–11pm, Sat & Sun 8am–10pm | Tip
The nearby museum at the Fashion Institute of Technology (FIT) has eye-popping, free
fashion exhibitions open to the public (227 West 27th Street, New York, NY 10001,
www.fitnyc.edu/museum).

75_Mothership

A throwback to the 70s' art scene opens her rooftop

In these days of chic, safe, and, face it, exclusive New York City, it can be hard to recall the 1970s when the city was about to go bankrupt. Muggings and murders were commonplace, and artists paid a pittance for sprawling cold-water lofts in abandoned SoHo factories. Certainly it was a much more dangerous city, but an atmosphere prevailed that attracted and nurtured innumerable artists, the likes of Andy Warhol, Patti Smith, Bob Dylan, and so many more of the creatives that are still today's cultural influencers.

A tiny remnant of that 1970s' art scene lives on at Mothership. This artist live-and-work space collective is housed in a permanently docked Brooklyn warehouse at the end of a gritty, industrial street that backs up to Newtown Creek. This ship that does not sail is a proud throwback to New York's art past and serves as a safe harbor where international artists can afford to anchor themselves in the 21st century.

Mothership has an open-house event on the second Tuesday of each month featuring artists of all stripes: filmmakers, performance artists, painters, sculptors, and so forth. When the weather cooperates, the guests migrate up the few steps to Mothership's spacious, unimproved rooftop. The evening becomes that month's variation of an open-air art party, as well as a blast from New York City's less stuffy, more avant-garde past.

Artists and non-artists are warmly welcomed at these casual events that require not much more than an open mind and a willingness to venture out to an edge of Brooklyn that might not be familiar, though is easy enough to find. The schedule can vary so please check the website for monthly events and surprises that Captain Sol Kjøk and her mates create. There is never a dull moment at Mothership, and when it's warm and inviting outside, the rooftop is open for expansive views while expanding your mind.

Address 252 Green Street, Brooklyn, NY 11222, +1 (718)389-8228, www.mothership.nyc, sol@kjok.nyc | **Getting there** Subway to Greenpoint Avenue (Line G), or bus B 32, B 62 to McGuinness Boulevard / Freeman Street | **Hours** 7:30pm on the first Tuesday of each month, weather permitting | **Tip** A real neighborhood joint for over 60 years, Peter Pan Donut & Pastry Shop is a ton of retro fun. Go for their delicious, classic donuts (727 Manhattan Avenue, www.peterpandonuts.com).

76 Night of Joy

A roof deck just like you'd build for yourself

Inviting friends over to hang out in your living room or, when it's warm outside, on your casual roof terrace would be a fun, low-key way to unwind after a long week. But, like so many Brooklynites, you live in a cramped apartment, possibly with roommates, and having your own roof deck is just a sweet fantasy. Or maybe you've been too busy to tidy up since, well, forever.

Either way, Night of Joy is the next best thing to having your own roof terrace. Downstairs, it's a spacious yet cozy and inviting living room-like space that just happens to have a long bar and friendly bartenders. Up just one flight of stairs is the casual roof deck, lit, planted, and decorated in a simple but festive way. A second bar on the roof serves delicious variations of New York's favorite warm-weather cocktail, the frozen margarita. Start the evening off at happy hour, which includes the fresh-fruit rooftop margaritas, daily between 5 and 8pm.

Locals, small groups, and revelers escaping the Downtown Manhattan bar scene – and even Tinder dates – make up the varied clientele. Night of Joy is also a second "living room" to many local musicians who come to hear the Wednesday and Thursday night DJ sets during which the unique playlist is selected by musicians.

Oddly, the rooftop at Night of Joy is not above the downstairs bar area, but rather above the adjacent hair salon. The roof deck is close to some of those very same cramped apartments mentioned above, so following good neighbor rules, the roof closes at midnight during the week and at 2am on weekends, and the amplified music is restricted to the downstairs bar. The open-air roof is shuttered when the mercury falls below 55 degrees; downstairs is always open until 4am.

Inviting and unfussy, and serving unique drinks infused with natural ingredients, Night of Joy is the indoor living room and outdoor roof deck of every New Yorker's dreams.

Address 667 Lorimer Street, Brooklyn, NY 11211, +1 (718)388-8693, www.nightofjoybar.com, info@nightofjoybar.com | **Getting there** Subway to Lorimer Street (Line L), to Metropolitan Avenue (Line G), or bus B 48 to Lorimer Street/Front Street | **Hours** Spring, summer, and fall Sun–Thu 5pm–midnight, Fri & Sat 5pm–2am | **Tip** You never know who might be performing at open mic night each Sunday from 5 to 8pm at Pete's Candy Store, Williamsburg's original live music venue since 1999, where Nora Jones, Rufus Wainwright, and many other talented musicians have performed (709 Lorimer Street, Brooklyn, NY 11211, www.petescandystore.com).

77__Northern Territory
Brooklyn's "outback" has a wide view of Manhattan

The Northern Territory in Australia is famous for its harsh deserts and famous red dome, Ayers Rock. Saltwater crocodiles, wombats, dingoes, and kangaroos live in and around the region's billabongs. In other words, it's an otherworldly place.

The manufacturing zone at the border of Greenpoint and Williamsburg is where you'll find the Aussie bar, Northern Territory. This used to be the "outback" of Brooklyn, full of interesting stuff but further away and not the big draw that North Williamsburg has become. However, once you venture to this unadorned former factory building, you'll be rewarded with a sweeping Manhattan vista from the casual second-floor rooftop. The drinks, compared to other rooftop bars, are cheap, and the menu is full of comfort food that pairs perfectly with a "few coldies in the arvo" (beers in the afternoon, in Aussie speak).

Northern Territory has two faces depending on the day of the week. From Sunday through Thursday, it's filled with low-key locals. On Fridays and Saturdays, however, the Manhattan crowd migrates across the East River to join the raucous, DJ-led, Aussie roof bar party. It's not unusual for guests to show up with a dozen or more of their mates for an impromptu celebration since reservations are not required and the roof is vast.

The indoor bar downstairs serves primarily as a gateway to the rooftop that draws crowds to this low-slung corner of formerly uninviting industrial Greenpoint. Northern Territory's rooftop bar has the frontier, casual backyard vibe of the vast region in Australia after which it is named. Here you can dash up to the roof for some fresh air anytime – even when it's raining. Choose your territory: on the weekends, come early for a big brekky (breakfast) and party until nighttime. Or meet up with the blokes and sheilas on a weekday to watch the sunset over the city with a cold one.

Address 12 Franklin Street, Brooklyn, NY 11222, +1 (347)689-4065, www.northernterritorybk.com | **Getting there** Subway to Nassau Avenue (Line G), or bus B 32 to Franklin Street/Meserole Avenue | **Hours** During warmer months, Mon–Fri 4pm–close, Sat & Sun 11am–close | **Tip** Around the corner at Acme Smoked Fish, they have been smoking fish for New York City for four generations. Each Friday for only five hours they sell their top quality smoked fish to the public – cash only (30 Gem Street, Brooklyn, NY 11222, www.acmesmokedfish.com).

78 __ Open House New York
The city opens its doors for one fun weekend

Unlike the accessible rooftops in this guidebook, there is one annual event that offers something slightly different: access to some of New York's *inaccessible* rooftops.

Beginning in 2003, New York City has held its great annual architectural weekend celebration, Open House New York (OHNY), a concept that originated in London. Over one jam-packed weekend each October, this citywide event allows the general public inside, or, in the case of roof explorers, on top of buildings with rare access.

Although the sites change annually, the listings always include rooftops. Past OHNY weekends have included tours of the nearly-impossible-to-visit formal gardens on top of Rockefeller Center, the many roof elevations, including a rooftop orchard, of the Via Verde housing complex in the Bronx, and the green roof at Pratt Institute in Brooklyn, as well as access into architecturally significant private homes with green roofs or rooftop gardens.

In order to control the crowds for the most popular destinations (and rooftops are always very popular), OHNY implemented a low-cost, online reservation policy for many of its sites. These spots often fill up quickly. A further complication is that the complete selection of hundreds of sites is revealed not long before the event. Therefore, getting the maximum roof exploring out of this brief opportunity requires a careful strategy only known to insiders: go to www.ohny.org as soon as it is updated, usually by mid-September.

Scour the listings for places that might have rooftop access and make your reservations (some sites may require a fee). Note the times when the rooftops are open (some are only open one of the two weekend days, or at specific times), and make your plans. Be sure to leave enough travel time from one rooftop destination to the next.

Rain or shine, OHNY offers exciting opportunities for rooftop exploration.

Address Across all five New York City boroughs, www.ohny.org | Hours One select
October weekend each year | Getting there See website for locations | Tip OHNY offers
tours to amazing inaccessible sites throughout the year to members, and funds go to
support their annual OHNY events. Consider joining this worthwhile organization to
take advantage of the membership benefits (www.ohny.org).

79 Ophelia

Frank Sinatra's regular Manhattan haunt

Revisit the post-World War I era, the roaring 1920s, when women earned the right to vote, art deco architecture represented an entirely optimistic view of a modern future, and New York City was the progressive American embodiment of the happy times ahead. When it opened in 1928, The Panhellenic Tower, a 26-story art deco masterpiece, was the tallest building in midtown. At East 49th Street and First Avenue, it towered over Manhattan, offering views of just about everything since no taller buildings existed to block the sightlines.

The first New York City skyscraper to be built by a woman and run by an all-female board of trustees, The Panhellenic Tower was a 380-room dormitory-style residential hotel for single college graduate sorority sisters. The 26th-floor solarium was their beautiful public space to relax, socialize, and greet their gentlemen callers.

Soon after the stock market crash, the lagging economy forced the tower to allow in non-sorority women, and in 1934, all paying guests, men and women, were welcomed. In 1940, when the building was rebranded as The Beekman Tower, the solarium was redesigned as Top of the Tower, a rooftop bar frequented by UN employees and celebrities such as Frank Sinatra and Pearl Bailey.

Top of the Tower closed in 2013 and reopened in 2018 as Ophelia, a stylish and sophisticated rooftop bar with two open-air terraces in what is now a landmarked building. Tall lancet windows that show off delicate inlaid ironwork, original black-and-white checked floor tiles, and a unique collection of antiques, some of them about The Panhellenic Tower, embellish the bar's interior. Updated and fresh, but with a clear connection to its roaring 1920s', feminist, and academic past, Ophelia is a brand-new version of an old New York destination with classic art deco design, superior views, and creative cocktails.

Address Beekman Tower, 3 Mitchell Place, 26th Floor, New York, NY 10017, +1 (212)980-4796, www.opheliany.com, info@opheliany.com | Getting there Subway to Lexington Avenue–53rd Street (Line E), to 51st Street (Line 6), or bus M 15 to First Avenue–Mitchell Place | Hours Mon–Thu 5pm–2am, Fri & Sat 5pm–4am, Sun noon–2am | Tip Tour the General Assembly Hall, the Security Council Chamber, the Trusteeship Council Chamber, and the Economic and Social Council (ECOSOC) Chamber at the UN Headquarters. Buy tour tickets online in advance (United Nations Headquarters, New York, NY 10017, https://visit.un.org).

80__Our Wicked Lady

Where the rooftop bar is only the beginning!

Located in industrial Bushwick, a neighborhood of low-slung, spread out warehouses, is a hidden-in-plain-sight slew of restaurants, studios, shops, and bars catering to Brooklyn's burgeoning artistic community. One of these formerly nondescript-looking buildings is now home to the neighborhood's only rooftop bar, Our Wicked Lady (OWL).

The artificial turf, picnic tables, sailcloth shades, string lights, white picket fence, and swimming pool blue wall invoke a touch of Miami on this tidy rooftop. At one end, there is a bar serving cocktails, beer, and delicious frozen alcoholic concoctions adorned with tiny paper umbrellas. At the other end of this cozy rooftop is the stage where bands, DJs, comedians, and performance artists can be as loud as they like until as late as they want since there are no sleeping neighbors nearby to lodge noise complaints.

OWL offers emerging talent a fun, casual, and attractive rooftop on which to perform throughout the outdoor weather months. Some shows are free while others require affordable tickets. Each Thursday night, OWL always charges something to attend as the door money and a percentage of the bar goes to the good charitable cause they have selected to support that month, often a music-related organization.

The roof is only part of OWL's holistic business. The grungy indoor bar and the suburban rooftop is one-third of the triad of interdependent businesses OWL's three owners have created. In half of this former warehouse are five artist studios and three band rehearsal rooms. When the artists and musicians finish a piece or practice session, they and their friends have a ready-made place to hang out, have a drink, and listen to some music. The bands that practice in OWL's rehearsal rooms sometimes perform there too, further solidifying OWL as a creative hub in this art-centric community.

Address 153 Morgan Avenue, Brooklyn, NY 11237, www.ourwickedlady.com | **Getting there** Subway to Morgan Avenue (Line L), or bus B 60 to Johnson Avenue/Morgan Avenue | **Hours** Mon & Tue 4pm–2am, Wed–Fri 4pm–4am, Sat 3pm–4am, Sun 3pm–2am | **Tip** One-of-a-kind hats and jewelry handmade locally with love are sold at Aileyan Accessories (257 Varet Street, Brooklyn, NY 11206, www.aileyan.com).

81_Penthouse 808

Feelin' groovy next to the Queensboro Bridge

In the 1990s, Mayor Rudolph Giuliani was busy cleaning up New York City. Strip clubs evicted from Times Square moved across the East River to gritty, industrial Long Island City. Then, a 2001 city rezoning law drastically changed that area. Suddenly, the under-10-minute subway commute from Rockefeller Center and the spectacular waterfront views of Manhattan transformed blue-collar Long Island City into a rapidly gentrifying neighborhood.

Almost two decades later, between the charming Queensbridge neighborhood park to the north, the historical Gantry State Park to the south, and in kissing distance of the Queensboro Bridge, lies Penthouse 808 atop the Ravel Hotel. More than a 10-minute walk from the subway through a still largely industrial neighborhood, arriving by taxi is a good option.

Penthouse 808 offers spectacular, close-up views of the Queensboro Bridge and her masonry towers. Built in 1909 and made famous by F. Scott Fitzgerald in *The Great Gatsby,* Simon & Garfunkel in the "59th Street Bridge Song (Feelin' Groovy)," plus countless movies, it's no wonder that romantic marriage proposals happen here.

Below is the landmarked New York Architectural Terra-Cotta Works building. To the left are enormous Con Edison towers that generate electricity for New York City. The East River, Roosevelt Island, and Midtown Manhattan are ahead.

An excellent Asian-fusion dinner menu is served under the retractable rooftop that opens for gorgeous summer evenings under the stars. Live jazz is enjoyed at the weekly Wednesday lobster bake and Sunday brunch. Happy hour cocktails and appetizers are offered each Tuesday through Friday from 5 to 7pm, when groups from jetBlue or Silvercup Studios pop by after work. Penthouse 808 has a full Bose sound system and transforms into a lounge on Fridays and a dance club on Saturdays until 3am. Zelda Fitzgerald would love it!

Address Ravel Hotel, 8-08 Queens Plaza South, Long Island City, NY 11101, +1 (718)289-6118, www.ravelhotel.com/penthouse-808 | **Getting there** Subway to 21st Street–Queensbridge (Line F), to Queensboro Plaza (Line 7, N, W), or bus Q103 to Vernon Boulevard/Queens Plaza North | **Hours** See website for seasonal and dining schedule | **Tip** While at the Ravel Hotel, the third-floor summertime rooftop pool at Profundo Day Club is an over-21 bit of Miami in New York City. Day and half-day passes are available all season long (www.ravelhotel.com/profundo-day-club).

82 Pier 15

Gorgeous double-decked pier with rooftop lawns

Sleek and urban, modern and inviting, with knock-out views in every direction. That's Pier 15. This pier juts out 500 feet into the East River, affording spectacular views of the Brooklyn Bridge and Brooklyn Heights. Look behind you for a panorama of the Lower Manhattan skyscrapers that comprise the Financial District (FiDi), or glance south to see the East River down to Governors Island. No matter where you look, it's fabulous NYC-flavored eye candy.

Pier 15 is part of the East River Esplanade, which starts at the bottom of Manhattan at the Whitehall Ferry Terminal, the Manhattan home of the Staten Island Ferry, and continues up the east side of the island for two miles. The Esplanade offers protected bike lanes, shops and restaurants, public art, and frequent ferries that take you as far as the Rockaways or nearby to IKEA in Red Hook.

The double-decked Pier 15 is a star attraction of the East River Esplanade. It offers beautiful gardens and rare river access on the lower deck. On the upper level are elevated lawns and breezy viewpoints. Ample, fun seating dots the pier everywhere: double-wide tropical hardwood benches on the lower level encourage people to snuggle up, while Adirondack chairs on the upper deck invite contemplation. Or choose to relax on single lounge chairs, traditional park benches, kidney-shaped seats, or amphitheater-style steps to enjoy the watery views and the birght sunshine.

Gorgeous all day, and more beautiful at night, Pier 15's elegance shines through even more brightly when the superbly well-designed lighting scheme turns on each evening. Even though the roof deck closes at dusk, plan to arrive just before then to enjoy the upper deck breeze as the sky darkens. Then head down to the lower level where the pier's artful lighting creates a tranquil riverside atmosphere where you can stretch out on a double-wide lounge chair until the clock strikes midnight.

Address East River Esplanade at South Street and Fletcher Street, New York, NY 10006, www.nycedc.com/project/east-river-waterfront-esplanade | Getting there Subway to Wall Street (Line 2, 3, 4, 5), to Fulton Street (Line 2, 3, 4, 5, A, J, Z), or bus M 15 to Water Street / Fletcher Street | Hours Daily upper deck 8am – dusk, lower deck 6am – midnight | Tip Sail the East River to New York Harbor on *Pioneer*, a beautifully restored 19th-century schooner, operating May through October (Pier 16, 167 John Street, New York, NY 10038, www.southstreetseaportmuseum.org).

83__Pier 62 Carousel

This green roof protects 33 cute native species

A 15-month-old child wearing her pink embroidered dress and clinging to her grandmother's chest, gazes with wide-eyed awe as the elaborate carousel creatures and the children riding them go round and round and up and down to the sound of music. This could be a scene from 1876, when America's oldest merry-go-round, the Flying Horses Carousel, was installed in Coney Island. Yet, nearly 150 years later, at the Pier 62 Carousel, this timeless scene is re-enacted daily between March and November.

While the Pier 62 Carousel continues the expected 19th-century traditions, it also innovates in several, very modern ways. Thirty-three hand-carved and painted animals adorn the ride, but instead of featuring horses, the creatures represented at Pier 62 are species native to the Hudson River Valley and the river itself. Riders can choose from sitting on the back of a beaver, a horseshoe crab, a striped bass, a green turtle, a peregrine falcon, or even a skunk. The ride can serve as the perfect segue to teach about the river's ecosystem. For little ones who might shy away from riding a black bear cub or coyote, one of the two white unicorns, the only non-native species, remains a popular choice.

At Pier 62, where traditional organ music has been updated to kids' versions of pop songs, what makes the Pier 62 Carousel unlike any other is what is *above* the revolving platform: a lush living roof bursting with native plants and solar panels that collect the sun's energy. Maintained by Hudson River Park Trust, the green roof gets watered each morning but otherwise survives on rainfall. The living roof will likely go unnoticed by little ones in pink dresses, but adults who understand the enormous contribution of green roofs to the health of New York City's infrastructure can see that what's above this carousel is as impressive as the timeless ride below.

Address Hudson River Park at Pier 62 between West 22nd and West 23rd Street, New York, NY 10011, +1 (718)788-2676, www.pier62carousel.com | **Getting there** Subway to 23rd Street (Line C, E), or bus M23 to West 23rd Street/West Side Highway | **Hours** Summer months daily 11am–8pm, check website during the rest of the year | **Tip** The Downtown Boat House offers free kayaking from May through September. Bring your own lock to safeguard your belongings in one of the free lockers (Pier 26, Hudson River Park between Huber and North Moore Streets, New York, NY 10013, www.hudsonriverpark.org/explore-the-park/activities/kayaking-at-pier-26).

84__ The Plaza

Fordham's Lincoln Center campus controversy

This 2.2-acre rooftop sculpture garden at Fordham University's Lincoln Center campus was called Robert Moses Plaza. A monument stood in the garden dedicated to Robert Moses, the former New York Parks Commissioner, because he secured the land for the massive redevelopment project that included building Lincoln Center and expanding Fordham University into Manhattan. In fact, Robert Moses was an honored speaker at the 1970 dedication of Fordham's Lincoln Center roof garden.

However, in the past five decades, while the towering trees, climbing vines, and lush gardens that make their home on what is now known simply as "the plaza" have matured, the contribution made by Moses is being re-evaluated. It's true that Fordham Lincoln Center would not exist without his vision, but in order to create the Manhattan campus and Lincoln Center, an entire socio-economically disadvantaged neighborhood was demolished, and thousands of people of color lost their homes and businesses.

Today's diverse Fordham student population and faculty are engaging in a conversation regarding how best to address the campus' history. Meanwhile, the plinth honoring Moses has been put into storage indefinitely. However, other significant sculptures and monuments are on exhibit, including the 28-foot-tall *Peter the Fisherman*. A circular grass lawn where students play sports between classes, and shady nooks for study, private conversations, or just lunch make The Plaza an oft-overlooked urban oasis.

The controversy behind this living roof is quickly forgotten as you enjoy the serene art, shade trees, flowering vines, and velvety lawns of Fordham's Lincoln Center Outdoor Plaza. Access the garden by stairs or elevator on Columbus Avenue near West 61st Street, or by the stairs tucked in-between the buildings on West 62nd Street, between Columbus and Amsterdam Avenues.

Address 140 West 62nd Street, New York, NY 10023, +1 (212)636-6000, www.fordham.edu |
Getting there Subway to 66th Street–Lincoln Center (Line 1), to 59th Street–Columbus
Circle (Line 1, A, B, C, D), bus M11 to Columbus Avenue/West 61st Street, or bus M10,
M20 to Broadway/West 63rd Street | Hours Daily | Tip Explore all corners of Central Park
on two wheels at Bike Rental Central Park. Ride around the 6-mile bike lane at your own
pace (892 Ninth Avenue, New York, NY 10019, www.bikerentalcentralpark.com).

85 Pod 39 Rooftop

Relax in a Mexican cabana on a reimagined rooftop

With its budget-friendly, pod-sized rooms, The Pod 39 hotel attracts guests with its fabulous public spaces, including their one-of-a-kind, 17th-floor rooftop bar. The elevator whisks visitors to a cozy, colorful, and comfortable indoor lounge area, and a short set of stairs transports guests to the century-old, spacious, and inviting open-air terrace. It's the near-perfect balance of old-world style and modern rooftop buzzy bar fun, attracting a primarily young and lively crowd all season long.

The style comes from one of the most famous architects of his time, Arthur Loomis Harmon. He worked in New York City's premier firm McKim, Mead & White before designing what was originally called The Allerton 39th Street House. Harmon later was a partner in the firm, Shreve & White, who built the Empire State Building. New York City had an affordable housing shortage back then too. The Allerton was designed as a cost-conscious residential hotel for working, single men, and acted much like a private club. In 1918, the rooftop oasis was the building's premier social area, just like it is today, although it's unlikely they were drinking tequila-driven cocktails served in baby watermelons back then.

The only Northern Italian Renaissance-style rooftop bar in New York City, Pod 39 Rooftop has been reimagined as a Mexican hacienda with a cabana-like bar set among the original Greco-Roman-style brick arches. Ivy grows up the weathered brick walls near the potted roses and mint, and strings of white lights add to the festive ambience. Seventeen floors above an already elevated Murray Hill street, delightfully cooling East River breezes and Manhattan views add to the pleasure. On chillier nights, a few weeks before and after summer, the Rooftop crew brings out standing heaters, allowing guests to enjoy this landmarked aerie for an extended season, no mater what the weather brings.

Address Pod 39 Hotel, 145 East 39th Street, 17th Floor, New York, NY 10016, +1 (212)865-5700, www.salvationtaco.com | Getting there Subway to Grand Central–42nd Street (Line 4, 5, 6, 7, S), or bus M 101, M 102, M 103 to Lexington Avenue / East 40th Street | Hours May–Oct 5pm–close | Tip Dag Hammarskjold Plaza is a living memorial to the United Nations secretary general who was killed in a plane crash on his way to negotiate a ceasefire during the Congo Crisis in 1961. The plaza is host to the lovely Katherine Hepburn Garden. A greenmarket every Wednesday serves the neighborhood (245 East 47th Street, New York, NY 10017, www.hammarskjoldplaza.org).

86 Premier57

Hot & bubbly rooftop pools at a posh Korean spa

Korean day spa fever appears to be highly contagious and is rapidly spreading across New York City. The *jimjilbang,* the Korean version of a hydrotherapy wellness center, is all about the ancient art of deep detoxing through sweating, scrubbing, relaxing, being with friends, and eating.

The swanky Premier57 spa offers six thematic saunas, including an ice room, gender-specific steam rooms, and all-gender warm pools. Exfoliating body scrubs and less traditional foot or full body massage, facials, and private suites for couples are available by reservation.

Premier57 is spread out over three floors in a modern Park Avenue office building near the sky-high pencil-shaped residential buildings that are rapidly changing the skyline of Manhattan. While muted marble and earth tones are the primary décor, once Premier57 turns on the lights, it can get very colorful. Mood-enhancing lighting schemes throughout the vast spa are designed with color or chromatherapy in mind.

The eighth floor's outdoor roof terrace has five separate warm-to-hot therapy pools. Three pools are built for one, two, or three people at most. Identical except for being adorned with different color tiles, green, yellow, and orange, they help guests continue the color-saturation treatment they may have started indoors, perhaps in the chromatherapy sauna or the infrared lounge. Next to the small round spas is the hydro spa that holds up to 10 people. The largest of the outdoor pools is divided into six individual bays, where guests rest against water jets in a space just big enough to comfortably spread out.

Get a day pass and plan on spending four to five hours traversing between the saunas, steam, indoor and outdoor pools, meditation room, sleeping room, and, of course, the delicious Korean café. Remember that the highly recommended exfoliating body scrub requires a reservation.

Address 115 East 57th Street, 8th Floor, New York, NY 10022, +1 (212)750-8800, www.premier57.com, info@premier57.com | Getting there Subway to 59th Street (Line 4, 5, 6, N, R, W), or bus M31, M57 to East 57th Street/Lexington Avenue | Hours Daily 9am–midnight | Tip Got Korean spa fever? Spa Castle New York in Queens is even bigger, though less luxurious. It has rooftop hot pools too (131-10 11th Avenue, College Point, NY 11356, https://ny.spacastleusa.com).

87__Queens Botanical Garden

Walk up this easy-access green roof

Just months before World War II began, the 1939 World's Fair in Flushing, Queens touted the slogan, "Dawn of a New Day." A five-acre botanical garden was one of the many popular exhibits. With community support, the tiny garden continued for 25 years until Robert Moses, New York's much-maligned "Master Builder," began planning the 1964 World's Fair in the same location. A man used to having his way, Moses had other ideas for this beloved plot of land. He bartered the original site for a nearby 39-acre site, now the permanent home of the Queens Botanical Garden (QBG).

Today, QBG has a mandate of environmental stewardship, and the $27 million Visitor & Administration Center exemplifies this commitment. The green roof and the building it covers earned numerous accolades soon after it opened in 2007, including a LEED Platinum rating, the highest rating given by the US Green Building Council.

Several features distinguish this 2,900-square-foot green roof, some obvious and others hidden from view. Designed with access for all, there are no stairs to climb, but rather a gently sloping, gravel-covered ramp. The roof is planted with native grasses and wildflowers, the right ecology for indigenous birds and butterflies. During a light rain, the green roof absorbs 100% of the precipitation but with heavier showers, rain overflows into the decorative ponds and fountains by the ground-floor entrance, reducing storm water runoff by an astounding 95%. Finally, the green roof insulates the auditorium underneath it, keeping it warm during winter and cool during summer.

Beyond the Visitor Center, QBG has 25 unique gardens. Use your olfactory sense on the Fragrance Walk; the essential oils of the shrubs and flowers are particularly strong. Or stop at the Bee Garden where plants attract those hard-working honey-makers.

Address 43-50 Main Street, Flushing, NY 11355, +1 (718)886-3800, https://queensbotanical.org | **Getting there** Subway to Flushing–Main Street (Line 7) | **Hours** Apr–Oct, daily 8am–6pm; Nov–Mar, daily 8am–4:30pm | **Tip** After your trip to the garden, take a walk through Flushing Meadows-Corona Park to see the Unisphere, the symbol of the 1964 New York World's Fair, and the Queens Museum, which from 1946 to 1950 was the temporary home of the United Nations General Assembly (New York City Building, Corona, NY 11368, www.queensmuseum.org).

88__RFTP

Pastel cocktails in pink flamingo sippy cups

The only thing about RFTP that is abbreviated is the name (ROOF-TOP minus three Os). Otherwise, it is long on seating with plenty of room at the bar, high-top tables, or numerous comfy lounge sofas. RFTP is also long on low-key fun. They maintain an easy, no-reservation policy, and many of the summery cocktails are served in hot pink, flamingo-shaped sippy cups sporting built-in, pink bendy straws. Pink flamingos also appear on the bartenders' Aloha-style shirts, worn as they concoct colorful cocktails, pour wine, or serve beer at the full bar.

Several vegetarian small plates are on the menu each evening. During the popular weekend brunches, healthy choices, such as a delicious shakshuka, are mainstays, though a tantalizing Nutella pizza might catch your eye.

The busiest times at RFTP are during brunch and the daily happy hour that starts when the rooftop opens at 3pm for three hours, with a very popular "Buy 1, Get 1 Free" drinks special.

Exiting the elevator on the fifth floor, guests cross a wooden bridge that echoes a beach boardwalk to enter RFTP. The open-air, L-shaped lounge has planters flowing with greenery along the lower section of the glass parapet. It is otherwise quite sparse, modern, and monochromatic, except, of course, for the staff's Aloha shirts and the smile-inducing sippy cups. If the pink flamingo cups and the pastel-hued cocktails just aren't your thing, beer is available on tap and in cans.

RFTP also has clever design features. The solar canopy above the bar creates very welcome shade on hot afternoons while it manufactures clean energy that keeps the bar humming. Views from the rooftop are seen through six-foot glass panels designed to keep noise in. A distant Manhattan skyline can be seen from RFTP but surrounding urban Williamsburg commands most of the vista from this modern hotel's welcoming rooftop lounge.

Address POD Brooklyn Hotel, 247 Metropolitan Avenue, Brooklyn, NY 11211, +1 (929)600-5588, www.rftpbrooklyn.com, info@rftpbrooklyn.com | Getting there Subway to Lorimer Street (Line L), to Metropolitan Avenue (Line G), or bus B62 to Driggs Avenue/North Fourth Street | Hours May–Nov, Mon–Fri 3pm–close, Sat & Sun noon–close | Tip Unearth old-timey treasures at Junk, a 5,000-plus-square-foot store brimming with vintage clothing, household items, furniture, and bric-a-brac (567 Driggs Avenue, Brooklyn, NY 11211).

89 RH Rooftop Park & Wine Terrace

A picture-perfect rooftop restaurant and wine bar

The Meatpacking District in Manhattan has a glamorous new resident, RH New York. Formerly known as Restoration Hardware, RH opened this six-story, 90,000-square-foot gallery, furniture, and lifestyle showroom that will dazzle you from the moment you enter the double staircase adorned lobby with the glorious crystal and light installation, *New York Night*, by artist and designer Alison Berger, to the glass elevator at the center of the store, past dozens of idyllic home vignettes, and up to the style-saturated fifth-floor rooftop restaurant and wine terrace.

RH New York's guests experience an exclusive world surrounded by the company's signature elegant and uncluttered designs. Each floor whispers luxury. And there are lovely food and drink options provided by restaurateur Brendan Sodikoff. The third level hosts a barista bar with an outdoor terrace. The top floor is home to a glass-enclosed restaurant and magnetically attractive open-air wine terrace, complete with panoramic downtown Manhattan views.

Pleasing architectural lines, a subtle water feature that creates soothing sounds, perfectly pruned matching London Plane trees, and sculpted Japanese boxwood hedges delineate the expanse of symmetrical groups of couches. The wraparound layout of the large RH Rooftop Park & Wine Terrace is a stylish oasis. It's an unhurried place to relax, visit with friends, or conduct business over a glass of summer rosé.

While the outdoor Wine Terrace menu is abbreviated, the grand, glass-enclosed, indoor restaurant offers beautifully prepared American cuisine. Breakfast, lunch, and dinner service will healthfully fortify shoppers for the rest of the immersive home lifestyle experience throughout RH New York's multiple floors of inspiring designs for living.

Address 9 Ninth Avenue, New York, NY 10014, +1 (212)217-2210, www.restorationhardware.com/content/category.jsp?context=NewYork | **Getting there** Subway to 14th Street (Line A, C, E, L), or bus M 11, M 12 to Hudson Street/West 13th Street | **Hours** Park & Wine Terrace is open in warm weather Mon–Sat 10am–9pm, Sun 11am–8pm | **Tip** When Bell Labs left its Manhattan home in 1968, this historic building became Westbeth, a professional artists' live-work community. Westbeth Gallery frequently exhibits residents' works that cannot be seen anywhere else (55 Bethune Street, New York, NY 10014, www.westbeth.org/wordpress/about/westbeth-gallery).

90 Riverbank State Park

The largest rooftop park in the western hemisphere

For more than 20 years, Harlem residents have stayed fit at this 28-acre rooftop marvel, but it didn't come easy. When New York City desperately needed a new sewage treatment plant and determined it should be built in Harlem alongside the Hudson River, local residents protested mightily, "not in my backyard." The city sweetened the deal by promising locals a new park bursting with recreational facilities *on top* of the treatment plant, and that is how the largest rooftop park in the western hemisphere came into existence. To comprehend its size, travel down the bike path to see that the park is actually 69 feet above ground level. Being well above the Hudson affords Riverbank State Park visitors advantages. There are unfettered views of the pristine New Jersey Palisades and a spectacular vista up river of the majestic George Washington Bridge.

Five major buildings are dotted throughout the park: an indoor Olympic-size pool, a covered skating rink for winter ice-skating and summer roller-skating, an 800-seat theater, a 2,500-seat athletic complex with a fitness room, and a 150-seat restaurant.

But with acres of rooftop at play, there is room for much more: an outdoor 25-yard lap and wading pool, four lighted tennis courts and basketball courts, a lighted softball field, four handball courts, a 440-meter, eight-lane running track built around a field that works for football or soccer, two playgrounds, a water-splash playground, picnic places, and a summertime carousel. There is even a rooftop community garden.

Scores of classes are offered for all age groups, including just about everything from belly dancing to chess instruction, painting classes to tennis coaching, and playing guitar to practicing Tai Chi. The Horticultural Society of New York also offers educational opportunities at Riverbank regarding plants and healthy living. Getting and staying fit is always easier in a beautiful environment.

Address 679 Riverside Drive, New York, NY 10031, +1 (212)694-3600, www.parks.ny.gov/parks/93/details.aspx | **Getting there** Subway to 145th Street (Line 1), or bus M 11 to Riverbank State Park | **Hours** Daily 6am–11pm; some of the facilities within the park are open seasonally or with limited hours | **Tip** Nearby, super creative Japanese-inspired cocktails served in eggshells and light bulbs are presented alongside ramen, a raw bar, and other Japanese delicacies at ROKC (3452 Broadway, New York, NY 10031, www.rokcnyc.com).

91 Riverpark Farm

Farming in Manhattan, one cubic foot at a time

Down a long driveway in the shadow of the storied Bellevue Psychiatric Hospital is one of the craziest farms you'll ever see. Riverpark Farm at Alexandria Center is mobile, it's on the roof of a parking garage, and it's adjacent to the FDR, the multilane highway that skirts the east side of Manhattan.

Riverpark Farm, however, is not the work of a lunatic. In fact, it is the carefully planned, lovingly tended, experimentation-friendly kitchen garden of the award-winning restaurant Riverpark. This modular farm is comprised of 3,400 double-stacked milk crates, each lined with filter fabric and filled with potting soil and compost. Each winter, the restaurant's executive chef and the Riverpark farmer pour through seed catalogs searching for miniature melons, heirloom tomato varieties, unusual herbs, edible flowers, and berries. Always up for trying something new, they are attempting to grow turmeric with plans to use the stalk and flowers as well as the bright yellow root with which we are familiar.

It's a daily occurrence for the just picked harvest to appear on a restaurant guest's plate an hour later, cranking up the "farm-to-table" concept into hyper-speed.

Easy to see, Riverpark Farm is surrounded by a low fence. To wander amongst the planted milk crates, ask a farmer, and if there is time, he or she will proudly show you around. Or if you're making a Riverpark restaurant reservation for lunch or an early dinner, request a farm tour. Alternately, the lush herb garden planted in the same style is located on the south side of the building and is always open to curious spectators.

Tables and benches invite a sit down, so bring a picnic or order some take out from the summer evening pop-up beer garden or Little River restaurant. Put in your earbuds to muffle the noise from the FDR and occasional helicopters and relax next to this inventive rooftop farm.

Address 450 East 29th Street, New York, NY 10016, +1 (212)729-9790, www.riverparknyc.com, info@craftedhospitality.com | Getting there Subway to 28th Street (Line 6), or bus M15 to East 29th Street/1st Avenue | Hours By appointment only | Tip Peer through the handsome wrought-iron fence at Gramercy Park, the only private park in Manhattan, to marvel at the enormous mobile sculpture by Alexander Calder (Gramercy Park East, New York, NY 10010).

92__ The Roof at PUBLIC
Your chance to experience the panache of Studio 54

Only the beautiful, outrageous, famous, or wealthy made it into Studio 54, New York City's ultimate 1970s' disco. Throngs of people waited outside every night, vying to be chosen to join the ever-changing, wild party inside. The force behind Studio 54's always fresh, outrageous, and nonstop adult-only fun was a then 30-something Brooklyn boy named Ian Schrager. Four decades later, Mr. Schrager is still creating excitement, but now, rather than running outrageous discothèques, he has evolved into a world-renowned hotelier.

Mr. Schrager's freshest hotel concept is PUBLIC, where luxury is no longer reserved for the wealthy but is available to everyday members of the public. His latest hotel creation in the Lower East Side, PUBLIC, has several accessible-to-everyone areas that create a variety of unique experiences, including The Roof.

This 18th-floor bar is a very sexy sunset and nightspot where guests are cocooned by only the most luxurious finishes: the acid-treated distressed Marine bronze bar that shines gold, the French black-on-black silk damask chairs, lots of granite and leather, and the Yves Klein blue LED lights that glow between the wide oak plank floorboards.

The floor-to-ceiling glass windows showcase New York City at night from the black and Yves Klein Blue interior year-round bar. The 2,500-square-foot outdoor terrace, open all summer, is decorated primarily in white and teak, and features a custom zinc bar. The terrace showcases all-around Manhattan vistas.

Getting into The Roof is as competitive as Studio 54, but keep a few tips in mind. Reservations are taken, but even if they are full, if you arrive early getting in is as easy as showing up. However, arriving late on a DJ night without a reservation might make you think you've traveled back in time to the 1970s when crowds waited outside the doors to nirvana at Studio 54.

Address PUBLIC Hotel, 215 3rd Street, 18th Floor, New York, NY 10002, +1 (212)735-6000, www.publichotels.com/eat-and-drink/the-roof, info@publichotels.com | **Getting there** Subway to Second Avenue (Line F), to Grand Street (Line B, D), or bus M 21, M 103 to East Houston Street / Bowery | **Hours** Mon – Wed 5pm – 2am, Thu & Fri 5pm – 4am, Sat 3pm – 4am, Sun 3pm – 2am | **Tip** Try some Montreal-style, hand-rolled, wood-oven-baked bagels and a shmear at Black Seed Bagels (170 Elizabeth Street, New York, NY 10012, www.blackseedbagels.com).

93__ The Roof at Whole Foods Market Third & 3rd

Putting the green back in green grocer

Groceries downstairs and craft beer plus seasonal fare upstairs makes The Roof a haven for food-loving Brooklynites, including many local chefs who frequent this rooftop restaurant and bar on their days off.

Many rooftops seem to have a transformative nature. During daylight hours, they are one thing, and when the sun goes down, they become something completely different. The Roof at Whole Foods Market Third & 3rd in Gowanus is no exception.

In the daytime, it's a family-friendly destination. Stroller-pushing parents from Park Slope can relax with a libation while the kids enjoy the indoor play area. It's fairly sedate; that is until Wednesdays from 10 to 11am when New York City's singing cowboy Hopalong Andrew arrives to entertain the delighted youngsters. During the evenings, the casual, after-work crowd arrives to drink, eat, or participate in trivia night on the roof.

Once the weather warms up, the glass garage door opens, and the shaded outdoor patio, adorned with wooden tables, benches, and flowering succulent plants, entices guests outside to enjoy the Manhattan skyline view.

This store was built by Whole Foods to very exacting environmental standards, and it has achieved a coveted LEED Platinum rating. The 400,000 recycled bricks from a former New Jersey factory, the graceful sculptural wind turbines adorning the parking lot, and the reclaimed wood from destroyed sections of the Coney Island boardwalk after Superstorm Sandy in 2012 give The Roof a cozy, been-here-forever feel. However, the store only opened in 2013 after a decade of soil remediation required by the Environmental Protection Agency because of its proximity to the Gowanus Canal Superfund Site. In spite of that, the food lovers of Brooklyn have fully embraced this rooftop destination.

Address 214 3rd Street, Brooklyn, NY 11215, +1 (718)907-3622, www.wholefoodsmarket.com/service/roof-taproom-dining-brooklyn | Getting there Subway to Carroll Street (Line F, G), or Union Street (Line R) | Hours Daily 11am–11pm; happy hour Mon–Fri 4–6pm | Tip If you want to do your socializing at home, pick up a bottle at Gowanus Wine Merchants. Stop by for generous tastings and choose from their impressive inventory of wines, spirits, sake, cider, and mixers (493 Third Avenue, Brooklyn, NY 11215, www.gowanuswines.com).

94 Rooftop 760 Copacabana
Legendary Latin club with a red hot salsa night

Since 1940, The Copacabana has been synonymous with New York City nightclub glamour. When it first opened on East 60th Street in Manhattan, the Latin beat, colorful Brazilian décor, Copacabana girls with pink hair and sequined costumes, and frequent celebrity sightings made it an instant hit with the style makers of the day. Top-shelf entertainers, such as Harry Belafonte, Sammy Davis, Jr., and Marvin Gaye performed at the Copa. Diana Ross & the Supremes debuted here. Dean Martin and Jerry Lewis were regulars. The club excited the imaginations of movie makers who included scenes from the Copa in many Hollywood films including *Goodfellas*, *The French Connection*, *Raging Bull*, and *Tootsie*.

After a half century, having survived the transition from Latin supper club to discothèque, the Copa moved to its second home on West 57th Street, and a decade later to its third home near the Javits Center on West 34th Street.

With the same owners and management team for decades, The Copa continues to draw in crowds. Today, in its fourth incarnation, this Copa, in the heart of the Theater District, is the first with an outdoor terrace called Rooftop 760. The retractable roof makes this 3,000-square-foot space comfy year-round, but when the weather is gorgeous, so is the nighttime view of twinkling New York City skyscrapers. At Rooftop 760, dance parties happen inside, under the fixed roof, but when your feet and ears need a break from the pulsating Latin beat, this club lets you take your drinks outside.

Rooftop 760 has a salsa dance party each Tuesday, cleverly called Salsa on 2'sDays, in reference to the dance style, Salsa on 2. Anyone over 21, even those new to salsa, are warmly welcomed.

For nearly 80 years, New York has been dancing at the Copa. In the legendary club's latest incarnation, partygoers can groove to the music inside and enjoy the fresh air outside at Rooftop 760.

Address 268 West 47th Street, New York, NY 10036, +1 (212)221-2672,
www.copacabanany.com | Getting there Subway to 50th Street (Line 1, C, E), or
bus M 20, M 104 to 8th Avenue/West 46th Street | Hours Fri & Sat 11pm–2am; Salsa
Tue 9pm–2am | Tip Restaurant Row begins across the street on West 46th Street
between 8th and 9th Avenues. Choose from more than 30 restaurants, from casual to
dressy, some with live entertainment and dancing nightly (www.restaurantrownyc.com).

95__Rooftop Films
Watch movies above Brooklyn and Manhattan

The Rooftop Films' Summer Series is a roof explorers' jackpot. Each year between May and August, visit as many as seven otherwise inaccessible New York City rooftops for this outdoor, avant-garde cinema festival. Scores of movies by emerging and established filmmakers are shown to tens of thousands of people in a huge variety of outdoor venues. They include everything from an historical cemetery to one of America's most famous beaches, a Park Avenue church, and even an artists' collective. But be sure to look for the following rooftop venues specifically (subject to change so check the website): Rooftop Films headquarters at The Old American Can Factory in Gowanus, Brooklyn; the Lower East Side rooftop of The New Design High School; two expansive rooftops at Industry City in Brooklyn; Brooklyn's Trilock Fusion Center for the Arts; the JCC Manhattan (see ch. 73); The William Vale Hotel in Williamsburg, and The Elevated Acre in Lower Manhattan (see ch. 39).

This nonprofit arts organization began quite by accident in 1997 when a recent college graduate set up an inexpensive sound system and hoisted a white sheet for use as a screen. He invited friends to the roof of the East Village tenement building where he lived and showed short films well into the night. More than two decades later, there are seven full-time employees and scores of dedicated interns and volunteers expanding this rooftop grassroots arts organization.

The movie is only part of the evening that Rooftop Films has in store for you. Several times per week, along with each screening, there is pre-film local live entertainment plus a happening after-party with live music. These events are reasonably priced and for an evening where it's best to get there early and stay late, it's a great deal – and a great deal of fun. Make sure to buy your tickets in advance, as they sell out regularly.

Address Suite E-106, 232 3rd Street, Brooklyn, NY 11215, +1 (718)417-7362, www.rooftopfilms.com, info@rooftopfilms.com | Hours May–Aug at dusk | Tip Czech That Film Festival at Bohemian National Hall shows fabulous foreign films on their spectacular rooftop, sometimes accompanied by live music (321 East 73rd Street, New York, NY 10021, www.bohemiannationalhall.com).

96_ The Rooftop at Pier 17

Introducing New York's 3,400-person rooftop venue

Cobblestone streets run throughout the oldest neighborhood in New York City around South Street Seaport. Once a bustling shipping hub where goods from all over the globe were bought, sold, and traded, there are so many layers of history here that each cobblestone in this historic district could probably tell a wild tale or two. The first people to live on this land were Native American Lenape. In the 17th century, this area became a Dutch commercial settlement. Later, when the English ruled Manhattan, it became a bustling world port where people from everywhere did business, worked, gambled, and caroused. Pier 17 became a tourist attraction in the 1980s, but during Hurricane Sandy in 2012, much of the historic Seaport district, including Pier 17, was heavily damaged.

During the pier's most recent rebuilding process, drawing locals back to the Seaport became a primary goal, so a new type of venue replaced the former touristy South Street Seaport mall. Today, a five-story building, with programmable, vivid light bands that vary the building's nighttime color scheme, juts 300 feet out into the East River. The new Pier 17 has a jam-packed, year-round rotating roster of events for all ages and interests. With multiple pier-level food and drink options, there is plenty of room for locals (and tourists) to enjoy the riverside vibe.

The main attraction at Pier 17, however, is on top of the building. Escalators whisk visitors to the open-air roof level, which is available for the public to enjoy whenever ticketed events are not scheduled. Views from this 65,000-square-foot public rooftop are so dramatic that they almost insist on being photographed. Unmatchable bridge and Brooklyn vistas day and night, free movies throughout summer, and a Winter Village, complete with ice-skating and hot cocoa vendors, make this 2.5-acre rooftop a must-see, year-round destination.

Address 89 South Street, New York, NY 10038, +1 (646)822-6990, www.pier17ny.com |
Getting there Subway to Fulton Street (Line 2, 3, 4, 5, A, C, J, Z), bus M15, QM11,
QM25, X15 to Water Street/John Street, or bus X8, X14, QM7, QM8, BM1, BM4 to
Water Street/Maiden Lane | Hours Dawn–dusk, when there is no rooftop concert or
private event | Tip Shop, eat, and enjoy the gallery at 10 Como Corso, the highly curated,
first US location of this posh store, gallery, and restaurant brand from Italy (1 Fulton Street,
New York, NY 10038, www.10corsocomo.nyc).

97 Rooftop Reds

Wine tasting at a rooftop micro-vineyard

Who needs miles of rolling hills in the countryside when you have a 15,000-square-foot rooftop in the Brooklyn Navy Yard? Clearly the creators of Rooftop Reds don't! The first-ever commercial rooftop vineyard has been established and is thriving.

The specially designed urban planting system consists of 42 custom-made aluminum boxes. Each weighs approximately 2,800 pounds and holds a total of 168 vines that will produce grape varietals for the first-ever commercial rooftop-grown wine.

As long as you're 21 years of age or older, you're invited to wander amongst the vines at this tiny boutique vineyard, and make sure to sample some wine at the rooftop tasting room stocked with an excellent selection of reasonably priced vintages from the Finger Lakes district in upstate New York. Devin Shomaker, founder of Rooftop Reds, studied viticulture, procured his grapes' root stock and serves wines from this little-known New York winemaking region.

Don't forget to hang out in the hammocks or luxuriate on the comfy outdoor sofas while taking in the unobstructed Manhattan views. They even have couples-sized red (of course) hammocks, perfect for rooftop canoodling. Special events, including sunset yoga, outdoor movies, and theme dinners happen with regularity. Free online reservations are required to gain entrance to the Rooftop Reds building in the Brooklyn Navy Yard.

The Brooklyn Navy Yard is enormous and can be confusing to newcomers, but finding Rooftop Reds is easier if you enter the Navy Yard at the Sands Street Gate. Go straight until the first fork in the road and then veer left. The brick warehouse in front of you is building 275. Enter through the double doors on the back side of the building. Wear comfy shoes – you've got more than 80 stair steps ahead of you to reach the rooftop vineyard and tasting room, a hike that is well worth the effort.

Address Building 275 (Sands Street Entrance), The Brooklyn Navy Yard, Brooklyn, NY 11205, +1 (703)582-8609, www.rooftopreds.com | **Getting there** Subway to York Street (Line F) | **Hours** Mar–Nov, Mon–Fri 4–9pm, Sat noon–10:30pm, Sun 2–8pm; check the website for special events | **Tip** Kings County Distillery (Building 121, 299 Sands Street, Brooklyn, NY 11205, www.kingscountydistillery.com), which ferments grain to make local moonshine, bourbon, and other whiskeys, is also located in the historic Brooklyn Navy Yard and hosts visitors on varying schedules.

98 Rosemary's

Where rosemary grows and sordid history happened

While executive chefs plan seasonal menus, Rosemary's executive chef designs the menu and the farm that will supply some of its coveted ingredients. Rosemary's sports a compact, rooftop farm that is easily accessible to its restaurant guests. Most attractive during the growing season when bursting with tomatoes, peppers, herbs, and flowers, this roof gives visitors the West Village vibe and view year-round.

Front and center is the ornate Victorian Gothic-style Jefferson Market Library and its adjacent jewel-like community garden. Built as the Third Judicial Court House in 1874, it's where Harry K. Thaw was incarcerated before his murder trial. Thaw shot Stanford White in 1906 (on a different rooftop!) when Thaw suspected his wife of having an affair with the philandering architect from the famous firm, McKim, Mead & White. From 1932 until 1971, the notorious New York Women's House of Detention stood next to the court house. The glorious Jefferson Market Garden now blossoms where once murderers and women of ill repute paid their debt to society.

If this seamy NYC history makes you hungry, you're in the right place. Rosemary's, a wildly popular enoteca (wine bar with small plates) and trattoria (a rustic, family-owned Italian restaurant) has an inviting, bucolic appeal with tiles, exposed bricks, natural wood, lots of light, al fresco sidewalk seating in warm weather, plus a happy hour on weekdays from 3 to 6pm.

The roof farm may look familiar as Rosemary's owner employed the help of Brooklyn Grange, New York's original commercial rooftop farmers, to create this "mini-Grange" using the same materials and methods, including composting and storm water collection. To supplement the roof-grown produce, Rosemary's has a farm 70 miles up the Hudson River Valley that provides more local produce and farm-fresh eggs for creating the chef's seasonal menus.

Address 18 Greenwich Avenue, New York, NY 10011, +1 (212)647-1818, www.rosemarysnyc.com | **Getting there** Subway to Christopher Street–Sheridan Square (Line 1), or West 4th Street–Washington Square (Line A, B, C, D, E, F, M) | **Hours** Mon–Thu 8am–11pm, Fri 8am–midnight, Sat 10am–4pm & 5pm–midnight, Sun 8am–4pm & 5–11pm | **Tip** Don't miss Mah Ze Dahr (Urdu for "the essence that makes something special") Bakery just three doors away on Greenwich Avenue (28 Greenwich Avenue, New York, NY 10011, www.mahzedahrbakery.com). Pete Wells, food writer from *The New York Times*, called their choux (vanilla-cream-filled pastry puffs with a surprise crackled, sugary cookie coating on the outside) one of New York's Top 10 Dishes of 2017.

99_ Rutherford Observatory

Look upward for the heavenly views

From most 15-story Manhattan rooftops it is thrilling to view the city below. But what the Rutherford Observatory, atop Pupin Hall at Columbia University, offers is the view above that can outshine even New York City with some heavy-hitting celestial competition. The view below is dominated by the neo-Gothic Riverside Church. At 392 feet, it is the tallest church in the United States. The bell tower houses a carillon with 74 bronze bells, including the 20-ton bourdon, the largest tuned bell in the world.

In spite of the spectacular view below, the crowd is drawn here every other Friday for the opportunity get closer to the planets, stars, and constellations above.

The Columbia Astronomy Public Outreach program holds a lecture and stargazing event twice a month during the academic year. The 30-minute lecture is followed by rooftop telescope observations, usually through one of three telescopes manned by the endearingly enthusiastic Columbia astronomy student volunteers. Inside the oxidized green rooftop dome, built in the 1920s, well before the surrounding light pollution began interfering, is a 14-inch Meade Schmidt-Cassegrain telescope. The volunteers focus the telescope and remain on hand to answer questions.

While rooftop visitors explore the enormous wonders of the galaxy on top of Pupin Hall, its underground laboratories are where 29 Nobel Prize laureates in physics studied the tiniest building blocks of our universe. In 1939, the first atom-splitting in the United States took place in the cyclotron in Pupin's basement. Furthermore, much of the early work on The Manhattan Project occurred at Pupin Physics Laboratories, and even our most famous wild-haired physicist, Einstein, did research here.

Take advantage of this opportunity to observe the heavens atop the building where the stars of the physics world have truly shined.

Address Pupin Hall, Columbia University Main Campus, New York, NY 10027, +1 (212)854-4608, outreach.astro.columbia.edu/calendar/index.html | Getting there Subway to 116th Street–Columbia University (Line 1) | Hours Sep–May alternate Fridays when classes are in session, lectures begin at 7pm or 8pm, stargazing begins at dusk | Tip Tour the impressive Riverside Church (90 Riverside Drive, New York, NY 10027, www.trcnyc.org) for free on Sunday, or for a small fee Wednesday through Saturday when reservations are suggested.

100__Sky Room
at New Museum
From bums to bohemians on the Bowery

For contemporary art and architecture, the New Museum is a haven. For unique views of Manhattan, Sky Room is an urban paradise! Each Saturday and Sunday, New Museum unlocks access to their seventh-floor event space, allowing museum-goers to see extraordinary views from the outdoor terraces. Elevator doors open to a stark white room with glass walls. Transparent doors lead to the L-shaped terrace that spans the south and east façades of the museum.

The Bowery, perhaps Manhattan's most storied street, is on the edge of five iconic New York City neighborhoods: SoHo, NoLita, the East Village, the Lower East Side, and Chinatown. From the Sky Room, you can see these unique neighborhoods, and further out to Lower Manhattan's Financial District, and across the East River to Brooklyn.

The New Museum opened on the Bowery in 2007, yet Bowery history began back when Europeans first settled in Manhattan. *Bowerij*, Dutch for "farm," reminds us that in 1651, Peter Stuyvesant, the first governor of the Dutch colony of New Amsterdam, purchased this swath of land far from the settlement of Europeans below Wall Street as a country farm. Much later, it became a crime-laden magnet for "Bowery bums," toughs, and women of ill repute. In 1955, 80 years after being in the shadow of the elevated railway, the Bowery was again exposed to sunlight and artists migrated here. Mark Rothko, Roy Lichtenstein, and Maya Lin are just a few who enjoyed cheap rent and a bohemian lifestyle among the flophouses and industrial shops on the Bowery.

When the New Museum chose this site next to the most famous of the flophouses, the Bowery Mission, even the architects were surprised at the unlikely location for a modern museum. But art continues to change this neighborhood, and today it is what Kevin Baker in *The New York Times Magazine* called a "hodgepodge of bohemia and business."

Address New Museum, 235 Bowery, New York, NY 10002, +1 (212)219-1222, www.newmuseum.org | **Getting there** Subway to Spring Street (Line 6), to Prince Street (Line R, W), or to Broadway–Lafayette/Bleecker Street (Line 6, B, D, F, M) | **Hours** Sat & Sun 11am–6pm; check the website for private events | **Tip** Walk west on Prince Street to Mulberry Street, where you'll find the NoLita Market, a weekend artisan and design market set up against the red brick wall of the St. Patrick's Old Cathedral graveyard (Prince Street between Mulberry and Mott Streets, New York, NY 10012, www.nolitaoutdoormarket.com).

101__ St. Cloud

Drink, eat, and luxuriate above Times Square

Sixteen stories above the hustle and bustle of Times Square is the stylish crown on a $250-million restoration of the landmarked Knickerbocker Hotel. John Jacob Astor IV built it for lavish partying in 1906, six years before he died on the *Titanic*.

Today, an elevator transports you to this 7,800-square-foot, year-round, indoor-outdoor bar nestled behind the Mansard-style roof and Beaux Arts façade. In keeping with the historical feel, the mixologists create vintage cocktails. Small plates designed by multiple Michelin-star-awarded chef, Charlie Palmer, are on the menu. A cigar lounge offering Nat Sherman's renowned tobacco products completes the sophisticated ambience.

By day, decorated in subtle hues of beige and charcoal, St. Cloud has a relaxed vibe. The blooming foliage and lush living green wall adorn the 3,400-square-foot outdoor bar, which sports three corner-hugging VIP Sky Pods. These semi-private lounges are surrounded by the original copper roof decorations and have the optimal vantage points to overlook Times Square. One of the Sky Pods offers the closest possible look at the Waterford Crystal ball and its annual descent that is televised to millions of viewers each New Year's Eve.

By night, St. Cloud takes on a different, sexier feel. As the theater district lights up, so does St. Cloud. Though there is no neon allowed on this landmarked building, the views of Times Square, the DJ, and the well-dressed clientele promise an evening like no other.

When Manhattan throws you a cold or wet evening, head to the indoor bar for an after-work drink and to enjoy the unparalleled wattage from above Times Square. Earlier in the evenings and earlier in the week, the ambient music remains in the background, but on weekends (which incidentally start on Thursdays in most Manhattan bars) and as it gets later, the music gets louder – and the crowd gets younger.

Address The Knickerbocker Hotel, 6 Times Square, 17th Floor, New York, NY 10036, +1 (212)204-5787, https://theknickerbocker.com/dine/st-cloud | **Getting there** Subway to Times Square–42nd Street (Line 1, 2, 3, N, Q, R, W), or 42nd Street–Port Authority Bus Terminal (Line A, C, E) | **Hours** Mon–Wed & Sat 4pm–midnight, Thu & Fri 4pm–1am, Sun noon–10pm | **Tip** Take the perfect selfie standing on the subway grate that blew up Marilyn Monroe's dress in the movie, *The Seven Year Itch* (Lexington Avenue and 52nd Street, New York, NY 10022).

102 __ St. John the Divine Vertical Tour

Behind the scenes at God's house

Imagine a house so big that the ceiling is twelve stories tall, plus the attic that adds another three stories, for a total of 168 feet in vertical height. This home's grand dome is made of Guastavino tiles surrounded by carved stone with ribbed vaulting. Clearly, this isn't just any house; it's a house of worship, the largest Gothic cathedral in the world, and the world's fourth largest church behind St. Peter's Basilica at the Vatican, Our Lady of Aparecida in Brazil, and the Seville Cathedral in Spain.

In 1828, St. John the Divine, cathedral of the Episcopal church in New York City, was conceived. Construction began in 1892, and to this day is not yet completed. The oldest section, the east end is Byzantine / Romanesque, and the west end, where you enter from Amsterdam Avenue, is clearly Gothic with "height and light" as the predominant features. The cathedral is shaped like a cross, and its Guastavino dome, which you will soon be above, lies at the intersection of the cross bridging the two architectural styles.

Intrepid roof explorers should wear closed toed shoes and be fit enough to hike up lots of stairs as the Vertical Tour takes you where non-clergy rarely go. Traverse the Triforium (the Bishop's Walk) and get sweeping Manhattan views from the roof of one of the flying buttresses that supports this massive structure. Dozens of spiral steps later, you reach "la-Forêt" (the forest) since in most churches, the enormous beams that hold up the roof are made of timber. Here, la-Forêt is made of fire-retardant steel beams as per city building codes. It is dusty and ill lit, but the back side of the dome is impressive, with the ingenious interlocking Guastavino bricks exposed, revealing the symmetrical convex shapes that made this structure possible.

Address 1047 Amsterdam Avenue, New York, NY 10025, +1 (212) 316-7540, www.stjohndivine.org/visit/daily-tours | **Getting there** Subway to Cathedral Parkway–110th Street (Line 1, B, C) | **Hours** Mon 10am, Wed & Fri noon, Sat noon & 2pm | **Tip** Before your vertical climb, take a much easier hike just across Amsterdam Avenue to fortify yourself with some delicious flaky strudel or poppy seed pastries and a cup or two of bottomless coffee at the cash-only Hungarian Pastry Shop (1030 Amsterdam Avenue, New York, NY 10025).

103___ Studio Café

Art, food, and endless views – American-style

Muse on American art in the largest open gallery space in a Manhattan museum. The spectacular new home of the Whitney Museum of American Art is exhilarating, but it can also be exhausting. Reaching the last gallery on the eighth floor, you've earned a sit down with a little something delicious to eat or drink. The Studio Café provides contemporary light fare and a full bar for museum-goers. Relax in the airy indoor space, or when the weather agrees, grab a seat at one of the tables under the enormous umbrellas on the east-facing terrace where 300-degree city views await you. With the Empire State Building in the distance, get a bird's-eye view of the Meatpacking District, West Village, and Chelsea neighborhoods while enjoying farm-to-table dishes and drinks so artfully prepared they might one day earn their own museum exhibit.

Studio Café takes up a small portion of the 13,000 square feet of outdoor exhibition space on three levels of The Whitney. The stairs, with cantilevered landings that connect the top three floor outdoor terraces, feels perfectly solid – until you look straight down a few hundred feet through the metal mesh and realize just how high up you are.

Gertrude Vanderbilt Whitney, an artist and great collector of American art, started The Whitney Museum of American Art in 1931. In 2015, this Renzo Piano-designed Whitney opened with great fanfare. Reflecting the industrial heritage of the area, the museum rises above the southern portion of the High Line (see ch. 53), the elevated freight rail line that is now an exquisite elevated ribbon park. At the bottom of what is now known as the Starchitect District, Renzo Piano's Whitney Museum is the first in a series of buildings adjacent to the High Line designed by many of today's most renowned architects such as Frank Gehry, Sir Norman Foster, Zaha Hadid, and Jean Nouvel.

Address Whitney Museum of American Art, 99 Gansevoort Street, 8th Floor, New York, NY 10014, +1 (212)570-3670, www.untitledatthewhitney.com/page/studiocafe, info@untitledatthewhitney.com | **Getting there** Subway to 14th Street (Line A, C, E), to 8th Avenue (Line L), or bus M 14A to Hudson Street/Horatio Street | **Hours** Sun & Mon, Wed & Thu 10:30am–5pm, Fri & Sat 10:30am–9pm | **Tip** Fat Witch Bakery in Chelsea Market sells their irresistible brownies at half price after 5pm each day (75 Ninth Avenue, New York, NY 10011, www.fatwitch.com).

104_ Tavern 29
Drink on the roof of a burned-down firehouse

When Boss Tweed ran 19th-century New York, fires were extinguished by private clubs that competed over "turf" and were quite corrupt. Not surprisingly, Boss Tweed began his political career as a gangland firefighter. A private firehouse from the period originally stood where Tavern 29 stands today. After the firehouse burned down, a respectable dentist converted the property into a four-story townhouse, where he raised his family. When Dr. Todd died, and as the neighborhood changed, the townhouse became a boarding house where Matylda Neiman, the notorious pickpocket, called by *The New York Times* "a beautiful girl," lived until she was nabbed by the police.

By the time of Ms. Neiman's arrest, the Silk District had taken over East 29th Street between Park and Madison Avenues, and the house was replaced by the two-story Silk Exchange Café in 1916. It served the neighborhood until the 1950s, when a wall-covering business moved in. In 1989, the building returned to its former life as a café, first as Red Sky and now as Tavern 29. The new owners updated the cozy rooftop, now tucked in-between taller buildings that have sprung up in the last 70 years. This New York-centric "biergarten" is open any time New York enjoys a warm evening – even on the occasional unseasonably warm mid-winter's day.

Tavern 29 has exclusive relationships with a Brooklyn and North Fork brewer, and they are the Manhattan hub for the small batch beers that can't be found anywhere else. Thirty-four draft lines are continually changing but are always focused on local breweries. Tavern 29 serves cocktails and the entire food menu on the roof as well.

Take a break from modern hotel roof bars at this neighborly rooftop destination where you can toast to a couple hundred years of tawdry New York City corruption and crime in the place where it actually happened.

Address 47 East 29th Street, New York, NY 10016, +1 (212)685-4422, www.tavern29.com, info@tavern29.com | Getting there Subway to 28th Street (Line 6), or bus M1, M2, M3 to Madison Avenue/East 28th Street | Hours Wed–Sat 11–4am, Sun–Tue 11–2am | Tip An easy 10-minute walk takes you to J. P. Morgan's luxurious personal office and library at the Morgan Library & Museum, which holds several Gutenberg Bibles and many other priceless treasures (225 Madison Avenue, New York, NY 10016, www.themorgan.org).

105__ Terminal 5 Rooftop

Two airport rooftops – visit one, view the other

JFK International Airport's redesigned Terminal 5 (T5) is the only place at New York City's three airports that allows all travelers who have passed through security to get some fresh air, and it's on a rooftop!

At JFK, the busiest of New York City's airports, T5 is one of six active terminals and handles over a million passengers each month. In response to the expanding demand to accommodate all who fly, jetBlue redesigned their T5 home to include an open-air rooftop terrace. Across from gate 28, this easily accessed space helps with the specific needs of traveling adults, kids, and pets.

Ten percent of the rooftop space is devoted to the T5 Wooftop, a terrific solution for pets' desperate moments. T5 Wooftop is a fenced-in, turf-covered section of the T5 Rooftop where pups can relieve themselves and run off-leash before or after flights.

Anyone who has traveled with young children knows that kids too can struggle with being cooped up in an airport or on a plane. To address that need, the T5 Rooftop designers covered another 10% of the outdoor space with bouncy, rubberized tiles so youngsters can play safely in the fresh air, like kids do.

Two turf-covered knolls invite travelers of all ages to stretch out near the lush plantings. The modern benches, bistro tables, and chairs create an ideal outdoor getaway in the post-security area. Free Wi-Fi extends throughout the terminal, including the T5 Rooftop, and shade is handily provided by the overhead skywalk that connects the AirTrain to T5.

Look closely when moving through the shade-making skywalk to see jetBlue's T5 rooftop farm. In thousands of attached one-cubic-foot milk crates, jetBlue grows veggies, herbs and, of course, blue potatoes. Once you've passed security, view the farm from two places: T5's Loft Kitchen Bar & Restaurant, or the fabulously fun jetBlue Jr. play area.

Address Across from Gate 28, Terminal 5, JFK International Airport, Jamaica, NY 11430, +1 (800)538-2583, www.jetblue.com/at-the-airport/terminal-5-at-jfk | Getting there Subway to Sutphin Boulevard–Archer Avenue–JFK Airport (Line E, J, Z), to Howard Beach–JFK Airport (Line A), then the AirTrain to Terminal 5, or bus Q3, Q10 to Terminal 5 | Hours Daily 6am–10pm | Tip Avid plane spotters know that the best places at JFK International Airport from which to see planes take off and land are on the top levels of parking lots 2 and 5 (JFK Airport, Jamaica, NY 11430, www.jfkairport.com).

106 __ Trapeze School New York

Be an aerialist on a Hudson River-hugging rooftop

You're about to jump off a 25-foot platform holding on just with your bare hands to a swinging wooden bar. Your mind is free from texting, social media, or daily worries. Ready to step off, your focus is clearly on what you are about to attempt in that moment as you stand on the outdoor platform situated about 100 feet above the Hudson River. You probably don't even notice the Statue of Liberty, Ellis Island, or One World Trade Center's 1,776-foot-high antenna just in front of you. And then you jump...

From April through November on the rooftop of Pier 40, Trapeze School New York offers a full aerialist curriculum, starting with small group classes for beginners through catch-and-release performance-worthy stunts for more advanced students.

Safety is paramount, and all trapeze students are belted in and tethered to one of three instructors that assist each class every step of the way. Anyone age six or over can get the adrenaline rush of stepping off the 25-foot platform and flying through the air. Those who've tried it claim it's quite addictive, which is possibly why this unique business has been thriving on Pier 40's rooftop since 2002.

If you catch the trapeze bug and need to fly through the winter season, you're in luck. Trapeze School New York offers year-round indoor classes at their Brooklyn location. But on a breezy summer's evening, the place to fly is on the roof of this multipurpose, multi-level pier.

Pier 40, located at the west end of Houston Street in Hudson River Park, is a sprawling community hub that serves many functions: it is a community rowboat house, a Hornblower cruise boat dock, a multilevel parking garage, and an urban mecca for soccer teams. It has public bathrooms, vending machines, bike parking, and, on its top level, it is home to the only rooftop trapeze school in New York City, and perhaps in the world.

Address Pier 40, 353 West Street, New York, NY 10014, +1 (212)242-8769, www.trapezeschool.com, info@trapezeschool.com | **Getting there** Subway to Houston Street (Line 1), or bus M21 to Washington Street/Houston Street | **Hours** Apr–Oct per class schedule | **Tip** Just south of Pier 40 is a Citi Bike dock, one of hundreds around the city. Buy a day pass and ride the 11-mile Hudson River Greenway, the scenic bike path that spans Manhattan from the Battery to the George Washington bridge. Note that you have to switch bikes every 30 minutes to avoid hefty surcharges (www.citibikenyc.com).

107 Upper 90 Soccer Center

Play pick-up games on two rooftop soccer pitches

Four billion fans across the globe make soccer the world's most popular sport. Queens is the most ethnically diverse region in the United States, where vast neighborhoods are populated primarily by people from soccer-loving countries in Central and South America and Europe. Plus, North American interest in soccer surged in 2010 when Team USA had a competitive World Cup team. In this setting, two friends began Upper 90 Soccer Center.

To grow as a retail business, it has to offer something extra. Upper 90 Soccer Center's owners understood this when expanding into Queens with their fourth store in 2017. They didn't want to just sell soccer balls, jerseys, and shin guards: they wanted to create a soccer-centric experience.

Upper 90's two-story soccer emporium in Queens has an indoor soccer pitch, a spacious café with top-shelf coffee and local pastries, and multiple screens that broadcast matches. The experience peaks, however, on the rooftop where two 40' × 80' open-air soccer pitches are ready for action.

Upper 90 Soccer Center offers a vast selection of soccer playing opportunities. While morning toddler open play sessions are at the indoor pitch so parents can take advantage of the café, the before- and after-work pick-up games, soccer camp, and adult co-ed and youth league games take place on the rooftop all summer long.

The turf-covered rooftop space at Upper 90 is so attractive that it has become a popular event space. When it's not hosting five-a-side tournaments, it might be used for birthday and engagement parties, or rooftop yoga and fitness classes.

Upper 90 has also created has also created an informal, international community center around the world's most popular sport in the heart of the most diverse region of New York City. This rooftop speaks with fluency the language understood by billions of soccer lovers.

Address 34-23 38th Street, Queens, NY 11101, +1 (646)863-7076, www.u90soccercenter.com, contact@u90soccercenter.com | Getting there Subway to Steinway Street (Line M, R), to 36th Avenue (Line N), or bus Q66 to 35th Avenue / 35th Street | Hours Retail store Mon – Fri 11am – 8pm, Sat 10am – 7pm, Sun 10am – 6pm; check website for rooftop events | Tip Just around the corner, learn about movie and television history and production at the fascinating and fun Museum of the Moving Image (36-01 35th Avenue, Queens, NY 11106, www.movingimage.us).

108_ Vida Verde

Surrounded by the colors and flavors of Mexico

As much as we love the intensity of New York City, sometimes we need a break from the traffic, the tourists, and the locals' devotion to wearing black. The Rooftop Margarita Market at Vida Verde offers no spectacular views of skyscrapers. Instead, it is a bright, modern, colorful escape from monochromatic Manhattan, hidden mid-block in the center of all the action.

Dominating the roof terrace is the spectacular spray-painted mural by celebrated, Mexican-born, Boston-educated graffiti artist Victor (Marka_27) Quiñonez, who is well known for bringing his eye-catching brand of street art to Disney, Converse, and other high-end advertising campaigns. This beautiful mural and the tropical greenery surrounding it instantly transport you away to a more relaxed place and pace.

Vida Verde is a creatively orchestrated symphony of colors and flavors, and the décor complements the beautifully prepared food. Tacos wrapped in fresh, house-pressed tortillas, made thick enough that they won't fall apart, are modern takes on Mexican food. Select the ribeye taco, the vegetarian Brussels sprouts taco, or for the food-adventurous, try the delicate flavors of the *huitlacoche* quesadilla.

The adventure continues at the bar with what is likely the deepest Mezcal menu in North America with 400-plus selections of this smoky Mexican spirit. There are also easy-to-drink frozen margaritas, including the classic lemon-lime and a beautiful pomegranate-hibiscus variety that suits the bright décor, as well as other colorful, delicious cocktails.

The roof terrace is designed for casual outdoor eating and drinking. While seating on the roof terrace is first-come, first-served, it is also a popular venue for private events. A quick call in advance will assure the rooftop is open to walk-ins at the time you want to go on your mini-getaway surrounded by the colors and flavors of Mexico.

Address 248 West 55th Street, New York, NY 10019, +1 (646)657-0565, www.vidaverdeny.com | Getting there Subway to 57th Street (Line N, Q, R, W), or bus M 20, M 104 to 8th Avenue / West 56th Street | Hours Daily 11 – 4am; rooftop closes at 10pm | Tip Find a Prohibition-style speakeasy behind the red velvet door, then down the stairs at Tanner Smith's (204 West 55th Street, New York, NY 10019, www.tannersmiths.com).

109_Westlight

So many roofs, so little time…

Looking a little more Miami than Brooklyn, a 23-story white-and-silver monolith to luxurious modernity rises out of this low-slung, formerly industrial neighborhood in the thick of gentrified Williamsburg. The fashionable William Vale Hotel sports four rooftops, three of which are public-access.

The hotel begins at ground level with 20,000 square feet of retail, including a lush, artisanal donut shop. That is covered by a second-story public-access roof park complete with a raised-bed mini roof farm. On the fourth-floor setback, hotel guests can enjoy the 60-foot outdoor swimming pool. There is plenty of in-building parking, a few more floors of meeting and event-ready rooms and 10 stories of state-of-the-art hotel studios and suites, each donning its own private terrace. Crowning all this well-appointed majesty are two extraordinary rooftop bars, the year-round indoor-outdoor Westlight and its seasonal all-outdoors sister, The Turf Club.

Twenty-two stories in the stratosphere and open year-round, Westlight offers its guests an array of bespoke cocktails, curated snacks, blown-glass lighting, star-chef-selected music, of the moment décor and, best of all, incomparable Manhattan skyline views. During the warmer months, Westlight's three-sided terrace entices up to 100 additional guests to the other side of the floor-to-ceiling glass doors to enjoy the comfortable furniture, look through the tower viewers (permanently installed binoculars on a stalk) and revel in the steady breeze off the East River, even during a sweaty NYC summer heat wave.

If you're looking for a more casual summer vibe, ascend the stairs to the 23rd floor's more intimate, sporty roof bar. The Turf Club's sprawling synthetic lawn hosts outdoor party games, and there are always more handcrafted classic cocktails, rare spirits, beer, wine, and endless views.

Address The William Vale Hotel, 111 North 12th Street, 23rd Floor, Williamsburg, NY 11249, +1 (718)307-7100, www.westlightnyc.com | Getting there Subway to Bedford Avenue (Line L), or Nassau Avenue (Line G) | Hours Mon–Thu 4pm–midnight, Fri 4pm–2am, Sat 2pm–2am, Sun 2pm–midnight | Tip Nearby Brooklyn Brewery (79 North 11th Street, Brooklyn, NY 11249, www.brooklynbrewery.com) offers free tours on Friday nights and every half hour on Saturdays and Sundays. Tours are free; beer is sold in the Tasting Room.

110_ Williamsburg Hotel

Swim at the pool bar or drink in a water tower

More luxurious rooftop choices exist in the Williamsburg neighborhood of Brooklyn than anywhere else in New York City, and in 2018, the Williamsburg Hotel added two more noteworthy beauties to an already impressive list: The Rooftop, a seasonal pool and lounge, and The Water Tower Bar, an all-season, late-night, exclusive lounge.

During the summer months, The Rooftop, a chic pool and bar area, is open for swimming and sunbathing from 11am to 5pm daily with purchase of a day pass. Be prepared to spend some more cash if you want to rent one of the stylish single or group-sized day beds or a cabana. Excellent casual food and drinks encourage guests to stay all day long. While not inexpensive, a stay-cation at The Rooftop is more affordable than, say, traveling to Miami, and offers a New York City rooftop rendition of the southern Florida pool party feeling.

After 6pm, when no more swimming is permitted, entrance to evening parties around the pool is free. On Thursday and Friday nights, a DJ gets the poolside party going, while on weekends, the day parties' beat extends into the late evenings.

For those seeking a less crowded, more sophisticated experience, there is another, super stylish, year-round rooftop option at The Williamsburg Hotel: The Water Tower Bar. Open only Wed–Sat 10pm–4am, and by reservation only, this modern lounge in the shape of a classic water tower is constructed of glass, wood, and steel. Holding not more than 60 people, The Water Tower Bar is expensive, exclusive, and impressive. Velvet couches and artwork by a local muralist define the luxe interior, while the widow's walk-style outdoor area around the circular bar affords twinkling, panoramic views of everything New York.

Chic and fun, or ultra-posh and sophisticated, The Williamsburg Hotel adds two gorgeous choices to the most rooftop-centric district in New York City.

Address Williamsburg Hotel, 96 Wythe Avenue, Brooklyn, NY 11249, +1 (718)362-8100, www.thewilliamsburghotel.com | **Getting there** Subway to Bedford Avenue (Line 7), to Nassau Avenue (Line G), or bus B 32 to Wythe Avenue/North 12th Street | **Hours** The Rooftop: Sun–Wed 11am–midnight, Thu–Sat 11–2am; The Water Tower: Wed–Sat 10pm–4am | **Tip** On the former Rosenwach Water Tower Factory site, where most of New York City's cedar water towers were once manufactured, now stands The Hoxton Hotel with two outdoor rooftop choices: Backyard is a casual terrace a few floors up, and Summerly is the delightful seasonal roof bar (97 Wythe Avenue, Brooklyn, NY 11249, www.thehoxton.com/new-york/williamsburg/restaurants-and-bars).

111 Yo Yoga!

Bliss out for an hour and breathe the air

Need a vigorous mind-body workout, or trying to stay strong and flexible? Try Vinyasa yoga. Are you a stressed-out New Yorker, experience chronic pain, or need help to recover from an illness? Try Restorative yoga. Or, as many do, practice both styles depending on what your body needs that particular day.

Yo Yoga! offers active Vinyasa and gentle Restorative classes that max out at 20 people. Rooftop sessions fill up quickly, so reservations are suggested. The studio owner wants every participant to feel that he or she has as much room as needed to spread out, so while the 1,300-square-foot rooftop could accommodate more mats, the classes are always comfortable and never feel crowded.

When the mercury hits 68 degrees, it's rooftop yoga season at Yo Yoga! In 2011, this intimate studio was the first in New York City to offer a regular roster of rooftop classes. Yoga is taught out-of-doors on the private, padded rooftop that is fringed with flowering potted plants and is partially shaded by the neighbor's overhanging mature tree.

At Yo Yoga! senior citizens to college students participate in both the active and restorative practices, and about a quarter of the students are men. Classes are taught by a rotating group of kind, patient, and experienced yogis, including the studio's owner, Rebecca, who sets the welcoming tone for the entire studio.

With genuine southern hospitality and full dedication to her business, Rebecca infuses Yo Yoga! with positive energy. When looking to start the studio, a rooftop was not foremost on her mind. But when she saw that this space in what seems like an unlikely Upper East Side location between 1st and 2nd Avenues on the third floor of a walk-up had an unused rooftop, she knew that Yo Yoga! had found its home. Physical health and mental bliss can be found on this hidden urban rooftop at Yo Yoga!.

Address 344 East 59th Street, 3rd Floor, New York, NY 10022, +1 (646)490-7790, www.yoyoganyc.com, info@YoYogaNYC.com | **Getting there** Subway to Lexington Avenue/59th Street (Line N, R, W), to 59th Street (Line 4, 5, 6), bus M 57 to First Avenue/60th Street, or bus M 15 to First Avenue/57th Street | **Hours** See website for class schedules | **Tip** Ride 250 feet in the air on the Roosevelt Island Tramway, the only one of its kind in North America. For one swipe on your Metrocard, wander through Four Freedoms Park and the rest of historical Roosevelt Island (59th East Street & Second Avenue, New York, NY 10022, rioc.ny.gov/302/tram).

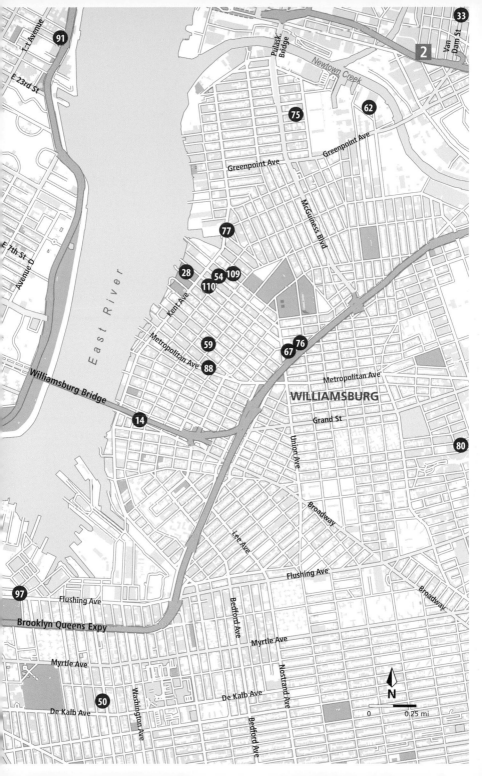

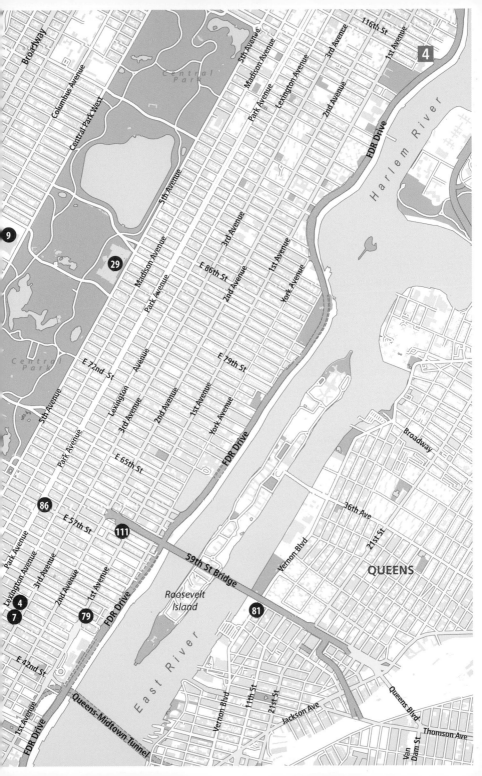

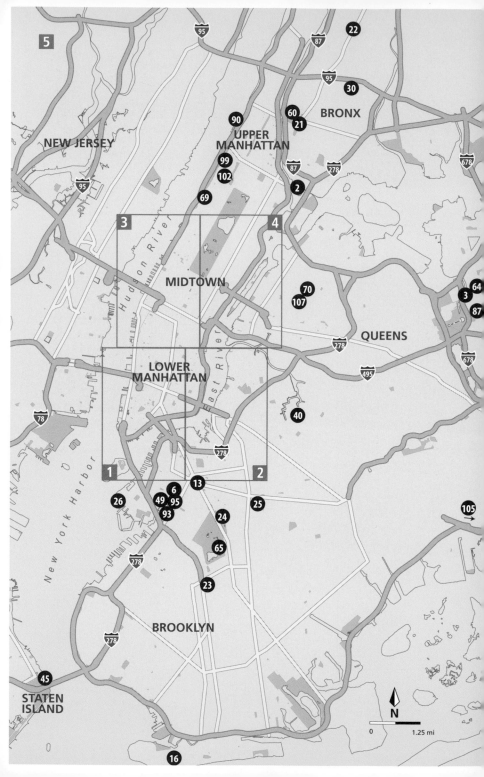

Michelle Madden, Janet McMillan
111 Places in Milwaukee
That You Must Not Miss
ISBN 978-3-7408-0491-6

Floriana Petersen
111 Places in Silicon Valley
That You Must Not Miss
ISBN 978-3-7408-0493-0

Joe Conzo, Kevin C. Fitzpatrick
111 Places in the Bronx
That You Must Not Miss
ISBN 978-3-7408-0492-3

John Major, Ed Lefkowicz
111 Places in Brooklyn
That You Must Not Miss
ISBN 978-3-7408-0380-3

Wendy Lubovich, Ed Lefkowicz
111 Museums in New York
That You Must Not Miss
ISBN 978-3-7408-0379-7

Andréa Seiger
111 Places in Washington D.C.
That You Must Not Miss
ISBN 978-3-7408-0258-5

Elisabeth Larsen
111 Places in The Twin Cities
That You Must Not Miss
ISBN 978-3-7408-0029-1

Joe DiStefano, Clay Williams
111 Places in Queens
That You Must Not Miss
ISBN 978-3-7408-0020-8

Allison Robicelli, John Dean
111 Places in Baltimore
That You Must Not Miss
ISBN 978-3-7408-0158-8

Amy Bizzarri, Susie Inverso
111 Places in Chicago
That You Must Not Miss
ISBN 978-3-7408-0156-4

Laurel Moglen, Julia Posey,
Lyudmila Zotova
111 Places in Los Angeles
That You Must Not Miss
ISBN 978-3-95451-884-5

Gordon Streisand
111 Places in Miami and the
Keys That You Must Not Miss
ISBN 978-3-95451-644-5

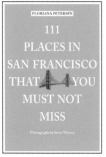

Floriana Petersen, Steve Werney
111 Places in San Francisco
That You Must Not Miss
ISBN 978-3-95451-609-4

Jo-Anne Elikann
111 Places in New York
That You Must Not Miss
ISBN 978-3-95451-052-8

Dave Doroghy, Graeme Menzies
111 Places in Vancouver
That You Must Not Miss
ISBN 978-3-7408-0494-7

Anita Mai Genua,
Clare Davenport,
Elizabeth Lenell Davies
111 Places in Toronto
That You Must Not Miss
ISBN 978-3-7408-0257-8

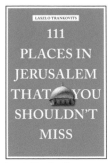

Laszlo Trankovits
111 Places in Jerusalem
That You Shouldn't Miss
ISBN 978-3-7408-0320-9

Christoph Hein, Sabine Hein
111 Places in Singapore
That You Shouldn't Miss
ISBN 978-3-7408-0382-7

Acknowledgements

I'd like to recognize Clay Williams who not only photographed this beautiful book but who kept me organized and informed, always with a smile on his face. Clay, you went way above and beyond – thank you! I'm indebted to Manny Velasquez who expertly critiqued each and every entry along the way; my mom, Ethel Adatto, who provides my safety net so I can do projects like this; and my son, David Pearl, who is my inspiration. Thanks also to Karen Seiger, my visionary book editor, whose determination made 111 Rooftops a reality.

– LA

This project was quite the undertaking, and Tammi Williams got to hear about nearly every moment of it - whether she wanted to or not. Thanks so much for listening. My love goes out to her and to the first ladies in my life, Sonia Williams, Heather Williams, Lois Nembhard and Sheena Williams.

As a lifelong New Yorker, I thought I knew this city inside and out. Many thanks to Leslie Adatto for showing me an entirely new perspective for seeing this place that I love.

– CW

The author

Leslie Adatto has been seeking out New York City rooftops since relocating to Manhattan in 2010. She blogs about New York City rooftops (lookingupwithleslie.com) and organizes two active Meetup groups, The New York Roof Deck and Roof Gardening Meetup Group and Rooftop Drinkers NYC. Leslie earned a BA in English from UCLA, is a former high school teacher and runs a bicoastal business. Leslie lives, bikes, and cooks in the West Village.

The photographer

Born in Queens, raised in Brooklyn, **Clay Williams** is a lifelong New Yorker who photographs food, drinks, and events for *The New York Times*, *Edible Communities* magazines, and the James Beard Foundation. With his camera in tow, Clay has hung on to the back of food trucks in Paris, trudged through farms in Argentina, and squeezed into tiny kitchens with world-famous chefs. When he's not documenting the food system, he's at home, cooking dishes inspired by what he photographs every day. Clay lives in Sunset Park, Brooklyn, with his wife Tammi, a fellow New York native.